INSPIRATION EXPLAINS
ITSELF

INSPIRATION
EXPLAINS
ITSELF

BY

JOHN B. CHAMPION, A.M., Th.D.

Professor of Christian Doctrine
Eastern Baptist Theological Seminary

"But there is a spirit in man, And the
inspiration (breath, neshamah) of the
Almighty giveth them understanding."
---Job 28 : 8.

"All Scripture is given by inspiration
(theopneustos, God-breathing) of God."
---II. Tim. 3 : 16.

WIPF & STOCK · Eugene, Oregon

Wipf and Stock Publishers
199 W 8th Ave, Suite 3
Eugene, OR 97401

Inspiration Explains Itself
By Champion, John B.
ISBN 13: 978-1-5326-1311-1
Publication date 10/21/2016
Previously published by The Evangelical Press, 1938

To

FOREWORD

THE thesis of this book is, the Bible manifests that it is God's Word when read by any who have a spirit similar to that which produced it. The Word might be used by a spirit utterly below its level. This would result in perversion or subversion of what it says, as with Satan in our Lord's temptation in the wilderness. When a man says, "The Constitution of the United States definitely teaches that the best form of human government is anarchy," evidently he is moved by a spirit far below that of this great document. When a pastor says to his prayer-meeting group on Christmas week, "The Scriptures definitely teach that Jesus Christ had a human father," he also is evidently possessed by another spirit than that of the Word. The Bible is the Book of the Holy Spirit. This it manifests to those led of the Spirit, "For as many as are led by the Spirit of God, these are sons of God" (Rom. 8:14).

This, then, is our theme, that the Word of God is strategic in our relations to Him and in the Christian life. To its health and fruit-bearing the Bible is indispensable. Holy Writ is the kind of thought and word which goes along with that kind of life. Instinctively the unbeliever realizes that it does not belong to the sort of life he lives. Let such rejecters of the Word say and do what they may, those who receive it as the Message of God are better off in every way, for they find the Oracles of God genuine and competent to originate and maintain right relation to Him, as far as teaching goes.

When any man would serve the Master *in His way,* the constant ministry of the Bible thereto becomes imperative. Let him lose faith in the Scriptures as the Word of God, and his power to win men to the Divine Salvation vanishes. Unless we come to some such faith in Holy Writ as the Holy Spirit has, He cannot take of the things of Christ and shew them unto us (Jn. 16:15). "Now the natural [unspiritual] man receiveth not the things of the Spirit of God: for they are foolishness unto him; and he cannot know them, because they are spiritually judged [examined]" (1 Cor. 2:14). The man who really abides in Christ, hungers for His Word. And no man prays effectually except as he is taught and incited by the Word. In His Divine wisdom the Son of God bound up together these three essentials of fruitful Christian living— Abiding in Christ, in His Word, and in prayer: "If ye abide in me, and my words abide in you, ask whatsoever ye will, and it shall be done unto you" (Jn. 15:7). This is the practical trinity of Christian living.

At a student-pastors' conference in our seminary not long ago a speaker said, when a student he had heard in one of our classes the professor proclaim the ideal for pulpit ministry. Evidently it worked, for this graduate stands in one of the most prominent pulpits in our land, in Tremont Temple, Boston. The statement was, "The only word which God promises will not return unto Him void, is His own. There is no guarantee that what we say even *about* the Scriptures shall prosper. Our job is to get across to the people the Word of God itself."

We have been passing through an age in which the Bible has been more diligently depreciated than exalted, more criticized than preached and practiced. No wonder that it has been a period of lessening regard for the Word; and no wonder that congregations have melted away in many instances, and evening services been abandoned or feebly maintained with a corporal's guard in place of the main army. All sorts of other attractions have been resorted to, while here and there the supreme attraction of the preaching of the Word of God from a pulpit on fire still succeeds. Imagine the pulpits of Wesley, Spurgeon, Brooks, or Moody being supplemented with picture shows, reviews of books, or lectures on current events!

Meanwhile the world-situation grows no better, rather worse. Wholly lost has been the lesson of the utter futility of the World War laying down eleven million lives and countless wounded and maimed, and trillions of dollars thrown away to make the world safe for democracy and for peace. Democracy does not seem to be prospering, and peace may have left for some other planet.

All this terrible failure could have been avoided by heeding the Word of God. Surely the feet of the image in Daniel's vision are still iron and clay not holding together. As prophesied this is a time of all sorts of disintegrations. Did not the Son of God tell us, "All they that take the sword shall perish with the sword"? (Matt. 25:62). How can we sow dragon's teeth and reap peace? "Be not deceived; God is not mocked: for whatsoever a man soweth, that shall he also reap" (Gal. 6:7). Do we not act as though we have more faith in shedding man's blood than in the shed blood of the Son of Man?

The Scriptures explain the Satanic complication of the situation. "We know that . . . the whole world lieth in the evil one" (1 Jn. 5:19). "The dragon, the old serpent, which is the Devil and Satan . . . that he should deceive the nations no more" (Rev. 20:2, 3). Surely only some malign supernatural power could push on the nations in inhuman aggression and in perpetual preparation for the slaughter of each other. Some laugh at this revelation of demonic influence, like the poor tubercular fellow gasping with his last breath, "I refuse to believe there is such a thing as disease." Many are fully persuaded that the suicide of civilization is in process. Do we refuse to be moved by wholesale preparation for and manufacture of still more terrible implements for wiping out millions of defenseless women, children, and noncombatants? What must be the end of this world-insanity? A demon-driven military machine has no ear whatever for the warnings of the Word of God, because as devoid of conscience as the demons themselves.

If we had trusted Christianization more and mere civilization less, this hopeless impasse before the nations might have been avoided. If it is too late to expect the nations to stop all this mania for vaster murder, with their hands either wet with each other's blood or getting ready to carry out the wild will of power-intoxicated dictators, it ought not to be too late to call all the followers of Christ to take counsel with God and turn unto the study of His Word as never before.

It is with this hope in mind that this little volume on Divine Inspiration has been written. Though its call may sound no louder than a sparrow's chirp, nevertheless it has encouraged the author to build like a swallow brooding nests of thought on the altars of the great Cathedral of the Divine Word. (Ps. 84: 3.) Earth and its civilization may pass in the dust and smoke of this insane conflict, but the message of the Book of Books midst it all will still be found teaching the Way of Salvation and Peace through the Prince of Peace and His servants—"the men of good will."

The material of this book comes from lectures on "Revelation and Inspiration" in the seminary course of Systematic Theology. I wish here to record my thanks for helpful suggestions from two of my esteemed colleagues, Professor William W. Adams, A.B., Th.D., and Professor David Lee Jamison, LL.B., Th.D. J. B. C.

CONTENTS

Part One

INSPIRATION IN INTRODUCTION

Introduction: The right of Inspiration to explain itself.

I. TERMS OF APPROACH TO THE SUBJECT
> The Meaning of Manifestation. Postulates of Personality. Apprehension as the objective counterpart to Manifestation.

II. THREE OUTSTANDING MANIFESTATIONS OF GOD
> Creation, Incarnation, and the Scriptures. The Incarnation by far the greatest Manifestation. To this the Scripture gives its testimony.

INSPIRATION, we believe, is competent to explain itself. It is a subject about which no man knows all. We are not omniscient in any matter. Fortunately, inspiration is from a Mind which does know everything. The Author of Holy Writ is omniscient. "His understanding is infinite" (Ps. 147:5). First of all it will be best to let Divine inspiration be heard in its own vindication. To contradict or repudiate that which he has not heard in interpretation of itself, does not lie in the mouth of anyone; and this all the more when its scope reaches away out far beyond that of the finite human mind.

I. Approaching inspiration's explanation of itself, we find grouped together these three closely related terms: *Manifestation, Revelation,* and *Inspiration.* In this word of introduction we may study the first of these, reserving the other two terms for the first chapter.

2   15

Divine Manifestation naturally prepares the way for Divine Inspiration, and in fact often coincides with it. His manifestation may be defined as any act in which God discloses Himself or furnishes information about Himself. Mainly, it emphasizes the Actor and His act. As a rule manifestation is more in deed than in word, but it may be in word. As a personal act of God it rests upon the same personal postulates which Revelation and Inspiration do. There are certain things which are self-evident in personal life. We may note a few of these.

Our first postulate is, that Divine Personality acts with meaning to Itself, for therein It lives, moves, and has Its satisfaction. The higher the life, the higher are its manifestations and satisfactions. Taking this personal point of view in our Theism, we hold that the Living, Personal God who has meaning in all He does, manifests Himself accordingly. He is always at work, as Jesus said: "My Father worketh even until now, and I work" (Jn. 5:17). All His works being indicative, they are bound to show something as to what kind of a God, Life, and Personality He is.

There is necessarily the complementary side to every manifestation. To be such it requires that it be made to some one. This may be called its objective counterpart. Because in His own image and likeness God made man, he was thus constituted as truly personal as God Himself; and man is therefore capable of perceiving and understanding the Divine manifestations, especially when these are designed for and adapted to man's understanding. Normally, manifestations of personal intelligence may be recognized by corresponding personal intelligence. This is all the more manifest when His Heart, Mind, and Nature conspire together in God's effort to interpret Himself. Personality, whether Divine or human, normally desires to be understood; and man shows himself to be normal in condition by welcoming such manifestation. He is abnormal when he acts otherwise.

II. There are three great outstanding manifestations of God: *in Creation, Incarnation, and the Holy Scriptures.* Because God is perfect in Personality He is not interested in merely imparting information about Himself. He is far more concerned in awakening and cultivating personal relations with those to whom His manifestations come. This is shown in the measure of these three great ways or methods to make Himself understood.

Of these three manifestations the greatest by far is that in "the Word made flesh." To the exceeding greatness of this manifestation the Scriptures bear witness; and in them the Personal Manifestation of God in Christ is *central.* As the Apostle John said: "The life was manifested, and we have seen, and bear witness, and declare unto you the life, the eternal life, which was with the Father, and was manifested unto us." "Herein was the love of God manifested in us (in our case), that God hath sent his only begotten Son into the world that we might live through him." "He was manifested to take (or bear) away sins." "To this end was the Son of God manifested, that he might destroy the works of the devil" (1 Jn. 1:2; 4: 9; 3:5; 3:8). Thus inspiration tells of God manifest in Person—the revelation of the vicarious, sacrificial love of God. There is also the promise of a coming and completing manifestation; "For the earnest expectation of the creation waiteth for the manifestation (revelation) of the sons of God" (Rom. 8:19). This is the full and final perfection and glory of Divine Redemption in Life Eternal.

I

REVELATION AND INSPIRATION

Introduction: Revelation defined and located.

I. THE PLACE AND THE DERIVATION OF INSPIRA-
TION
The Emphasis of Inspiration. Inspiration not always revela-
tion.

II. INSPIRATION CONSTITUTES THE SCRIPTURES
GOD'S MESSAGE TO MAN
This preëminent characteristic if ignored, serious results
follow. Why God chose inspiration as His method of communication.

III. THE SUBSTANCE OF THE HOLY SCRIPTURES
Law and Grace cover practically its whole story. Not the
lack of information causes men to remain lost, but lack of
disposition to use this knowledge. Dr. Strong's helpful
comparison of Inspiration, Revelation, and Illumination.

REVELATION is a general term for information furnished. In its derivation the word means an unveiling
or unfolding. It may be defined as the act of making
something known, or in its result it is the information
imparted. A Divine revelation is therefore something
which God discloses. While everything He does has
its own revelation, not all His acts are primarily intended for revelation. Only when His foremost purpose in any activity is to disclose or make known, may
it be properly termed a revelation.

I. *Inspiration is a special term either for a particular mode of communication or the message thus communicated.* In its derivation it comes from a verb

19

meaning "to blow" or "to breathe upon." It too may be either product or process, but the main emphasis of inspiration is on its process, whereas the main emphasis of revelation is on its product.

We may here note that the material of inspiration is not always revelation. For example, Moses wrote the story of Israel's journey from Egypt, which he and they already knew. As he was told by inspiration to do it, he included or excluded various matters as directed by God. "And Jehovah said unto Moses, Write this for a memorial in a book" (Ex. 17:14). In an epistle Paul repeats part of this same story which Moses had written, adding the explanation: "Now these things happened unto them by way of example; and they were written for our admonition, upon whom the ends of the ages are come" (1 Cor. 10:11). Because of his purpose in writing to a friend, one may include things already known to this friend; or he may intend the letter to be passed on to others. Even so inspiration may use many things already known, including them in its message. Because of this, while the Bible all came by inspiration, not all of it is revelation.

II. Here the tremendously significant and important fact should be taken into account: *Inspiration is the chosen Divine method which constitutes the Scriptures God's message to man.* Because in its most prominent feature the Bible is a Divine message, there is a written record of it to transmit and preserve it. Since Holy Writ is God speaking to us, it stands out in magnificent uniqueness among books.

By inspiration God has manifested His purpose to dedicate this Divine Message to *the immeasurably important end of originating, directing, cultivating, and perfecting the life of personal relation to Himself*. His Holy Spirit and the Word are two most powerful factors in keeping the religious life strong and useful to Him. If we lose sight of this preëminent characteristic of the Bible as a Divine Message, the main clue to its meaning and interpretation is gone. This is the very genius of its inspiration, that God is speaking to us by the Scriptures. When this God-given Book, as no other book can be, loses its meaning as a Divine communication to us, its inspiration will be surely stumbled over, assailed, or ignored.

Evidently the reason why God chose inspiration as His method of transmitting the Word to us, is because it is the way best adapted to communicate what He has to say to us. Does anyone know of a better way? Inspiration is the Divine adaptation to emphasize the Divine desire for the living relations to Him that we call the religious life. The Bible itself tells us what "pure and undefiled religion is," and is itself the great God-given means of keeping us "unspotted from the world" (James 1 : 27), by telling us the will of the Lord and how to live it with the utmost helpfulness and consecration. While our formal definition of inspiration is reserved for later and fuller discussion, we may here say in simple fashion, that Holy Writ is taken to be the means by which the Mind, Word, and Will of God are made available to us, inasmuch as we need indispensably its "light unto our feet," for who walks straight without it as "a lamp unto our path?" (Ps. 119:105).

III. *In substance the Scriptures present to us Divine Law and Grace.* This covers practically the whole story of God's outreach to save and sanctify man. In the message of Redemption we find His personal manifestation in the self-revelation of God in Christ, for "In him dwelleth the fulness of the Godhead corporally" (Col. 2:9, Douay Ver.). Both manifestation and revelation were present in His Incarnation; and both were unique, boundless, and therefore exhaustless. The Word presents His death as the Divine solution of the deepest and darkest of all problems, that of sin. Our Redemption has two main aspects— Godward fulfilment and manward mediation. Both of these also are boundless and exhaustless. God's message to man is, that the One and Only Way to Him is Jesus Christ. Sinners may remain lost after hearing of this. Then it is not so much lack of further information which causes men to remain unsaved, but lack of the disposition to act upon the knowledge already available. Alongside of the story of God's wondrous Grace manifest in Christ, is that of sin unmasking itself in its treatment of Christ. No man's sin is one whit better in nature than that which crucified the Son of God; for all sin seeks the death of the son-of-God-nature in us. Summing up we may say, Inspiration brings to us the Manifestation, Revelation, and Illumination as to how to be delivered from the delusions of iniquity into freedom through receiving and becoming all God has for us in salvation and its sequences.

Some find it difficult to discriminate between Inspiration, Revelation, and Illumination.   President A. H. Strong has helpfully compared them as follows:

  I. Inspiration without revelation, as in Luke 1:1-3.
 II. Inspiration including revelation, as in Revelation 1:1, 11.
III. Inspiration without illumination, as in 1 Peter 1:11.
IV. Inspiration including illumination, as in 1 Cor. 2:12.
 V. Revelation without inspiration, as in Exodus 20-22.
VI. Illumination without inspiration, as in modern preaching.[1]

[1] *Systematic Theology*, p. 197; Judson Press.

II

INSPIRATION AND THE MIRACULOUS

Introduction: Being nothing if not miraculous, Inspiration raises the whole matter of the miracle. The natural integrated in the physical realm. The natural in relation to the supernatural. Christianity, the Miracle, and Inspiration all in the same category.

I. THE POSSIBILITY OF THE MIRACLE GROUNDED IN THE ABILITY OF THE PERSONAL GOD
The Divine right to intervene in His own world. The need of man such that a perfect God must intervene to deliver him.

II. THE MIRACLE WROUGHT BY A POWER AND INTELLIGENCE NOT OF THIS WORLD
The power said to be Supernatural. The Personal God is not only supernatural but ultra-supernatural. Natural adjuncts used in the miraculous. All nature together insufficient to perform a miracle. God's immanence and transcendence. Theology recognizing the personal and transcendent God.

III. THE MIRACLE NOT INHARMONIOUS WITH NATURE
Distinction between law and force. The miracle no whim, caprice, freak, or prodigy. Misrepresenting the motive of the miracle not praiseworthy. The devotion to natural law objecting to the law of personal, Divine relation.

IV. THE MIRACLE MUST TAKE PLACE IN THE NATURAL REALM AND BY A POWER BEYOND IT
No miracle possible in heaven. Natural creation not a miracle. The corroboration of Scripture and human experience that miracles have taken place. The Miracles of Christianity not a liability but an asset.

V. THE MIRACLES OF CHRISTIANITY CONSISTENT WITH THE ATTRIBUTES OF GOD
Nature responded to Christ's miraculous power. Miracles wrought according to supernatural power and law. Na-

ture not more sacrosanct than God Himself. Nature not
absolute. Agnosticism, Deism, and Naturalism helpless.

VI. THE MIRACLES MORE TRUE TO MAN'S NEED
    THAN OBJECTIONS TO THEM
    The greatest miracle in Personality and in Act. The help
    of the miracle of the Incarnation. Miracles performed by
    Christ with perfect ease.

VII. CHRIST'S SINLESSNESS THE MOST LUSTROUS
     MIRACLE
     Ocular demonstration of miracles refused. Conclusions
     from the position that miracles are essentially incredible.

DIVINE inspiration is nothing if not miraculous. It
comes from the supernatural source of the Holy Spirit.
For this reason the study of the Inspiration of the
Scriptures is bound to bring up the whole matter of
the miracles. We may as well consider them here as
elsewhere.

By natural revelation we mean that which Nature
makes. Nature itself is the product of the supernatural; for God created it. However, He is not one
kind of God in the natural, and another in the supernatural. Trench says: "The miracle is not a greater
manifestation of God's power than those ordinary
and ever-repeated processes (of nature); but it is a
different manifestation." [1]

Anything natural is such because it is integrated in
the physical universe. The supernatural belongs to
the spiritual world above and beyond the natural. Between the two worlds there is no impassible barrier;
and God is at home in either. He is the God of the
natural as truly as He is the God of the supernatural.

---

[1] *On the Miracles*, p. 11.

There is that which is natural to the supernatural world or Person. Inspiration by the Holy Spirit is an activity natural to Him; and is as supernatural as He is. The supernatural and personal is capable of inspiring the natural. Christianity is fundamentally a religion of the supernatural, even as Jesus said: "My Kingdom is not of this world" (Jn. 18:36). The Christian life is a reciprocity of the natural with the supernatural. But the miracle does not come merely from the supernatural. It is from God who is greater than both worlds, and dwells in both, and far beyond them; as Solomon said, "Behold heaven and the heaven of heavens cannot contain thee" (1 Kings 8:27).

Christianity, the miracle, and the Inspiration of the Holy Scriptures are all in the same category; for each is essentially an interposition by God in Person in the natural realm to do that which the natural of itself could never do. God's Grace is the Divine down-reach of His love achieving that which natural law cannot do, in that it is weak compared with His Almightiness. This intervention does not displace natural law, and cannot interfere with it, for natural law cannot presume to regulate the personal activity of God. There are seven considerations of the validity of the miracle we wish to present here in order.

I. *The possibility of the miracle is grounded in the ability of the Personal God to intervene in His own way in His own world.* So to do is clearly His right, for this is grounded in Nature being His by Creation and Preservation. Since Nature came from Him and is sustained by Him, it cannot preclude or exclude Him from doing in it what He wishes. He would be other than perfect, if He did not desire to act in keeping with His personal relation to those whom He made in His own image and likeness, especially when they are in a strait so sore that nothing but His personal intervention could meet their need of deliverance.

II. *Manifestly the miracle is wrought by a power and intelligence not of this world.* The agency of the miraculous is really more than supernatural, for God in Person is as much above and beyond the supernatural world (usually called heaven), as He is above and beyond the natural. Usually it is said the miracle is performed by a supernatural cause. If, however, God Himself does it by His own personal power, this force is both supernatural and ultra-supernatural. In the process of the miracle natural adjuncts are not excluded. Christ made wine; but He used water. He fed the multitude; but He used a few cakes and fishes. In any case the miracle cannot be explained as due merely to natural causes. All the powers of nature combined are not sufficient to perform a solitary miracle. For example, all natural causes together could not have raised the dead body of Jesus Christ, and transformed it into an immortal body in place of His mortal one.

Of necessity, miraculous causes transcend the resources of the natural realm. While God is immanent in this world, His immanence is not an integral and organic part of it. A theology recognizing the transcendent nature and power of Divine Personality does not need to be coaxed into recognizing also the possibility it includes, that He may enter the natural realm to perform the miraculous. He would not be God at all, if without the personal possibilities, powers, and privileges so to do. By the technicalities of naturalism He is little likely to be turned back from coming to the help of those needing Him supremely and indispensably. Let us note that it is not the possibility of some single miracle which is at stake, but the whole ministry of the many miracles of Divine Redemption.

III. *The Miracle is not inharmonious with Nature.* The same power of God who made this world, is not rendered inharmonious to it by acting miraculously within it. Working a miracle does not cause the slightest contravention, contradiction, obstruction, or suspension of any natural law in the essential regularity of its operation. Law is not the force itself, but the uniformity with which a force acts. To change or interfere with natural law, there would have to be change of the nature manifesting itself in the force in which the law resides. The nature and force back of the Law of Gravitation were not in the least interfered with by the power superior to that of gravity when Jesus walked on the water. A special order of the personal activity of God cannot be in the least degree opposed to the regular order of the activity of the natural force which He instituted and has sustained from the beginning. The Divine cannot be either unnatural or anti-natural, for the natural and its force were constituted by God. All continuity of Nature is because of Him.

The charge that His miraculous intervention is whim, caprice, freak, or prodigy is sufficiently refuted by the fact of the dignity, perfection, and holiness of His Person. It is surely a wild derangement of thinking which in the name of God calls His interventions these names. Instead of this there should be flaming indignation with the actual intrusion of iniquity which is really both unnatural and anti-natural. Insane persons usually turn on those nearest related and to whom they are most indebted. It is not sanity which refuses to see that the necessity of miracles has come because of the invasion of sin, and that the intervention of Grace hinders nothing good and opposes nothing but evil, just as Grace was not opposition to the Law of God, but came to oppose instead spiritual death.

Surely misrepresenting the meaning and motive of the miracles of God is inexcusable. To put Him in the category of Unrighteous Intruder because of His gracious intervention is anything but fair and commendable. Instead, this ministry of love on any true ethical basis should be regarded as praiseworthy. To come with miraculous means to meet the rampage of sin on earth is just what naturalism is utterly incompetent to do. *It redeems no man from sin.*

The profound devotion to natural law which some profess, is as though it had saved them. If they would carry their devotion to law a bit further, and allow God the freedom of *the law of His personal relation and activity* on behalf of man in the toils of sin, it would be at least consistent. No matter who or how many mistaken ones object to it, the justification of the miraculous is in the need it meets and the unity it obtains. The miracle is embedded in the sacrificial grace of God who seeks to mend the disorder of evil and end the disharmony of iniquity and this, through personal union with Himself. Much more right has the miraculous grace of God to intervene in this world's wretchedness and confusion than has naturalism to object to it. Anti-miraculous objections have none of the power for good which God's great miracles of grace have. Such objections to the better cannot be for the best.

IV. *Of necessity, the miracle must take place within the natural realm though by means of a power beyond it,* yet not operating contrary to its laws. No miracle is possible or needed in heaven, there being no sin to cause the necessity of it. But heaven and the supernatural world are not wholly the same, for in part of the supernatural realm sin has intervened, as inspiration tells us. There, however, only supernatural or spiritual law reigns; and according to the Parable of Dives and Lazarus there is no intervention of grace for the lost in Hades. When God created this world, it was not by a miracle, for there was no natural realm at that time in which to intervene. Technically, the creation of Adam and Eve was part of the institution of this world, and need not be called miraculous, though it was supernatural.

Both the teaching of the Bible and the testimony of human experience corroborate each other that in this natural realm miracles have taken place. The Old Testament and the New are abundant in witness thereto. One is often asked why miracles so abounded at the beginning of Christianity. Perhaps as young transplanted trees need supporting stakes, so the supernatural character of Christianity was helpfully attested to by these supernatural interpositions. Some would reply to this by asserting that miracles are a liability and not an asset. Then Christianity itself would be a liability, for it began with the miracle of the Incarnation, and its great triumph started with the Resurrection of Christ. The rebirth of every life once broken by sin is a miracle-asset to any community in which it occurs. Denials of the miracles by that supernatural power of the Holy Spirit which still produces "the new creation" in Christ Jesus, cannot so blind us to the riches of His Redemption as to lead us to class them a liability and not an asset.

V. Next we may note that *the Miracles of Christianity are perfectly consistent with the Attributes of God*. The inspiration of the Scriptures, redeeming grace, and all the other supernatural assets of Christianity are in keeping with God's holiness and gracious nature. Nature itself has readily responded to the miraculous, even as the waves and the winds immediately obeyed "The Master of oceans and earth and skies." Those who saw this miracle did not question its reality. Instead they inquired, "What manner of man is this

3

that even the winds and the sea obey him?" (Matt. 8:27).

Those making the futile objection that miracles are not wrought according to the laws of nature, do not realize this is why they are miracles. They operate according to higher law of higher nature and power. The fact is that both the spiritual and the physical realms are in harmony with each other, except where there is the confusion and evil of sin. Nature should not be pictured or rather caricatured as a "touch-me-not" affair to God, more sacrosanct than God Himself. Were it necessary, many reasons might be given why He did not plan and build this world in such a way as forever to shut Himself out of it. Manifestly He created it with full prevision and provision for His immanence and personal intervention as occasion might require. May we note that time is not stopped when the hands of a watch are turned backward or forward (which is as a miracle to the watch); and no damage is thereby done to the works of this timepiece, because it is made to allow for just that sort of intervention. This world of human personality is equally designed for, not only constant personal relation of God in it, but also for His special intervention according to exigencies and the behest of His love and the wisdom of His will.

Deistic, Atheistic and other abnormal views, judged from the personal viewpoint, may represent Nature as sufficient in itself, that is, *absolute*. That such views are very far astray may be seen in the inherent, unescapable necessity which lies embedded in the very

constitution of the religious life and nature of man on
the one hand, and on the other the Personal nature of
God which desires to reciprocate in active relation with
man. That there is an extraordinary need of Divine
intervention to extricate and redeem man from sin may
be plainly seen in its perverse presence and desolation
of destruction. Deranged Deism puts God utterly beyond this world; and pictures both as mutually exclusive of each other. For such an iniquity-infested
and war-bedevilled world as this, anti-miraculous
views manifest tragic inadequacy to provide for the
immeasurable and desperate need of far more than
nature's help. It is considered inhuman to leave the
poor unconscious "drunk" in the ditch in zero weather.
That, however, leaves but one to hopelessness, while
Deism, Naturalism, and anti-miraculism means hopelessness for all and forever.

VI. Forgetting all temporizing theories and taking
all available facts into account, *nothing proves more
true to humanity's actual need and situation than the
sacrificial nature of God bestowing the miracle of His
saving Grace.* Nothing better or more completely befits the Divine character than the Miracle of the Incarnation and all the other blessed miracles following
in its train. That God could and did interpose miraculously to provide for the incomparable need of
man's restoration, is exactly the Father whom Jesus
Christ revealed. This same sinless Saviour is the
greatest miracle in personality. And the greatest miracle in act was Christ's revelation of what the Transcendent God actually is in heart, disposition, desire,

and sacrificial devotion. Men have strangely balked
at the miracle of Jesus walking on the water, and at
the same time have accepted His revelation of what
God is, not realizing that this is His supreme miracle
with the utmost of the transcendent in it and unfolding
what lies in the Divine nature, purposes, and possibilities for man's well-being. Surely this is "straining at
a gnat and swallowing a camel," yea, a whole herd
of them.

The infinitely marvelous miracle by which the pre-
existent Son was personally adapted and instituted
into human life, leaving His rank, place and glory at
the right hand of God, kenotically stepping down to
the state of a servant, and obediently suffering the
death-sting of sin that He might thus produce, so to
speak, the anti-toxin serum of Redemption from out
the life-blood of His Person, is fully in keeping with
the sacrificial Spirit of God who uses miracles great
or small in His divine economy because they so well
serve the aims and purposes of His redeeming love.

We do well to remember that to the Son the supernatural was as natural as the natural is to us. While
at tremendous cost of personal transformation by self-
limitation He brought His supernatural nature to
where He breathed the same air with men, yet never
in His incarnate life did He struggle to perform miracles. To do them was to Him as easy as to breathe:
"He breathed on them and saith unto them, Receive ye
the Holy Ghost" (Jn. 20:22). With the same perfect
naturalness He wrought His supernatural deeds, and
uttered His supernatural truths about God, Life, and

Immortality. His consciousness of superhuman power was manifest when He said, "If I by the finger of God cast out demons . . ." (Lu. 11: 20.) "They brought unto him many possessed with demons: and he cast out the spirits *with a word,* and healed all that were sick" (Matt. 8: 16). With the most perfect naturalness He uttered the miraculous words of closest intimacy with the Father in heaven which, as already said, revealed Him with more of the transcendently miraculous than any deed of healing the sick or of raising the dead. Surely His own enhumanation, His revelation of the Father, His resurrection from the dead are miracles stupendous, vast, and valid enough to let through and into this world all the lesser miracles recorded in the Bible.

VII. *Perhaps the most lustrous among the many miracles of our Lord is His sinlessness.* A few have attempted to refute the fact of His flawlessness; but no one is living as He did—without sin. Contemporary critics could not point to a single wrong He did, which enabled Him to say: "Which of you convicteth me of sin?" (Jn. 8: 46). Some like Hume may hold that a miracle is so contradictory to human experience, no amount of testimony in favor of it can be reasonably believed. A German philosopher is reported as saying that he would not believe a miracle, though he saw it with his own eyes. Then "Seeing is not believing" to such an one who refuses pointblank "ocular demonstration." Those who repudiate the trustworthiness of their own faculties are far from being impartial and trustworthy witnesses. All they prove is the incompetence of their evidence, for they have far more reason to deny the validity of their conclusions in this matter than to deny the validity of the miracle. But not only eyes can bear witness to this work and wonder of God. One has far more than his eyes to trust to if he would realize the proof of the perfect purity and Deity of Christ when He miraculously imparts the Holy Spirit to those who have long been dead and buried in iniquity. Then the miracle is within. There it is most convincing of all.

To hold that miracles are essentially incredible, is itself incredible. Then Christ should have seemed incredible to Himself, and refused to believe in practically all He did for others. And on this basis the Bible ought to be held the most incredible of books, the most unbelievable record in all literature. Is not this *reductio ad absurdum?* In beautiful pure reasonableness Jesus said, "If I do not the works of my Father, believe me not. But if I do them, though ye believe not me, believe the works" (Jn. 10: 37, 38). The spirit of unbelief is cast out only by a stronger belief and spirit, and not by mere argument.

Mad blindness which will not see the perfectly visible, must be left in its darkness. For the reasonable and truth-heeding person cause and effect correspond in any realm. Plainly Jesus Christ was, said, and did that which natural causes are wholly inadequate to explain or to produce. Natural law is limited to effects governed by the power moving in it. Therefore it cannot limit what the transcendent, Living God may do. Our necessity is God's opportunity to come as omnipotent as He is, and as miraculously as He does.

III

CURRENT THEORIES OF INSPIRATION

Introduction: Help of the Holy Spirit needed rightly to interpret Divine Inspiration.

I. CURRENT THEORIES DISCUSSED
The Intuitional theory. The theory of Illumination. The Plenary. The Dynamical. The Dictation. The Verbal. Dr. Warfield's position.

II. THE TWO EXTREME VIEWS COMPARED
These are the Dictation and Inspiration of Thought alone. A true view must be located between these extremes. The two great phases of Process and Product. The latter to be discussed first.

THE Bible itself bears witness that the ministry of the Holy Spirit has brought to us the Book of books. Rightly to interpret and use such a Book we need the help of the same Spirit who produced it. A Yale professor has facetiously said, the greatest discovery he made in forty years of teaching, is the ability of the average student to resist information. Much greater is the ability of the average sinner to resist divine information. And "All have sinned and come short of the glory of God" (Rom. 3:23).

When we find God speaking personally to us in the Holy Scriptures, we also hear the Holy Spirit bidding us pass on the message to others. To do this would show that we understand the Word and that the Holy Spirit is with us. As some one has said, when God's great gift of the Holy Spirit came at Pentecost, the disciples did not seek to rent that upper room, and proceed to hold a series of holiness meetings, but went forth everywhere preaching the Gospel.

I. SOME CURRENT THEORIES

One could go almost everywhere in discussing all the theories of inspiration which have been offered. Even to enumerate all of them would be more tiresome than informing. But we may glance at a few of the current interpretations to introduce our study of the subject of Biblical inspiration.

Like the poor, Naturalism is ever with us. Fortunately its tidal wave in our own day is now receding. One of its prominent explanations of inspiration is known as the *Intuitional* theory. As might be expected, this entirely ignores the supernatural. But inspiration by mere natural intuition is like theism with God left out. That Holy Writ has been produced by man's own unaided powers, is naming an utterly inadequate cause for the marvelous effect of the Word of the Living God.

Similar to the preceding theory is that of *Illumination*. According to this explanation as stated in the terms of modern psychology the human mind is sufficient, when illumined, to discover all the Divine truth contained in the Scriptures. But the Word of God is most profoundly a Divine message; and a message is given, not discovered. Clearly it would take more than human illumination however good to produce the revelation of the Mind of God which He has made in His own Word. Further, it not only reveals the Divine heart and desires but also His will concerning us.

Moreover, it is the Divine explanation of the way of salvation; and it records the exceedingly precious promises of God to those who trust and obey Him. The Bible itself serves to illumine the mind of man on all such subjects, but no illumination apart from the Bible could lead to the discovery of all the material which is in the Word of God, for such is utterly beyond mere discovery. Surely this is not how the Scriptures came together, that illumined minds found all its substance lying around waiting for some bright soul to discover it. This theory also holds that the Bible contains the Word of God, but is not itself that Word, just as some say, Christ is the most God-filled man, but is not God in Person.

The *Plenary* is a true and helpful statement as to the extent of inspiration, but offers nothing more to explain its process. According to it the Scriptures are inspired throughout, that is, equally in all their parts, though not of equal value in all their material. In this connection President A. H. Strong has wisely remarked that there are degrees of value but not of inspiration, even as there are no degrees of completeness; and completeness of inspiration is just that which the plenary theory asserts.

President Strong, Dr. Henry C. Sheldon and others have favored the *Dynamical* theory. A weakness of this explanation is its vagueness, for power alone does not explain the nature, process, and product of inspiration, just as power alone would not explain regeneration. This view holds that only the ideas of the Bible are inspired and that inspiration does not extend to the language expressing the thought of Scripture. Dr. Sheldon has said that inspiration is not mechanical. Grant it! But how can we substantiate this with only an undefined dynamic to define inspiration? Moreover, arbitrary separation of inspired thoughts from their inseparable words is mechanical in both spirit and method. Here are both Professor Sheldon's ideas and language: "Inspiration energizes rather than suppresses its subject. That is, inspiration must be dynamical rather than mechanical." [1] But the Inspirer Himself ought not to be suppressed; and is it not suppression of the Holy Spirit when He is shut out from sharing in the selection of the language upon which the thought He would express, must depend?

Evidently President Strong was not wholly satisfied with the Dynamical theory, even though he defined inspiration as "supernatural, plenary, and dynamical," for he went on to say: "Neither this nor any other theory is necessary to the Christian faith, inasmuch as revelation precedes inspiration." Yes, sometimes; but not when revelation comes by inspiration, of which much of the Bible is an evidence, and which he himself shows, citing Rev. 1: 1, 11. Dr. Strong's dissatisfaction with his own and all other theories of inspiration is manifest in saying: "Perhaps the best theory of inspiration is no theory." [2] This conclusion means that the best explanation of inspiration is no explanation at all. Yet some definite explanation of it we must have, or abandon the subject altogether.

---

[1] *System of Christian Doctrine*, p. 141. The Methodist Book Concern.

[2] *Systematic Theology*, p. 211. The Judson Press.

Professor Benjamin B. Warfield has treated this subject far more explicitly. He held the *Verbal* inspiration theory which he sharply distinguished from the *Dictation* theory. The latter he repudiated on the ground that it reduces the Biblical writers to mere amanuenses or automatons, who are pens but not penmen. He says:

"The Church, then, has held from the beginning that the Bible is the Word of God in such a sense that its words, though written by men and bearing indelibly impressed upon them the marks of their human origin, were written, nevertheless, under such an influence of the Holy Ghost as to be also the words of God, the adequate expression of His mind and will. It has always been recognized that this conception of co-authorship implies that the Spirit's superintendence extends to the choice of words by the human authors (verbal inspiration), and preserves its product from everything inconsistent with a divine authorship—thus securing among other things, that entire truthfulness which is everywhere presupposed in and asserted for Scripture by the Biblical writers (inerrancy)." [3]

"It is to be remembered that we are not defending a mechanical theory of inspiration. Every word of the Bible is the Word of God according to the doctrine we are discussing; but also and just as truly, every word is the word of man." [4]

Because of the importance of Dr. Warfield's statements on this matter before us another of his definitions is herewith added:

"By a special, supernatural, extraordinary influence of the Holy Ghost, the sacred writers have been guided in

---

[3] *Revelation and Inspiration*, p. 173. The Oxford University Press.
[4] Ibid, p. 419.

their writing in such a way, as while their humanity was not superseded, it was yet so dominated that their words became at the same time the words of God, and thus, in every case and all alike, absolutely infallible." [5]

II. THE TWO EXTREME VIEWS COMPARED

While a discussion of the verbal phase of inspiration follows this in Chapter Four, we may here say, there are the two extreme positions taken in this matter. The first is, that God left the writers all to themselves in selecting the words to express the inspired thoughts He gave them. The second is that the Holy Spirit dictated to the writers every word of the Bible. Surely a satisfactory statement will lie somewhere between these two extremes.

The Dictation view means that the writers were not inspired at all. No one needs to be inspired to receive dictation. It may be well to notice at this point that the Divine and the human being in coöperation in inspiration are not separable, for apart from each other there is not, and cannot be, any true Biblical inspiration whatever.

It will not prejudge the matter to point out here that in genuine inspiration there is bound to be sufficient room allowed for the coöperation of both agents, the Divine and the human. If the word "complicity" could be regenerated so as to have a good sense instead of an evil one, it would accurately describe the relation of this coördinate Divine-human activity in inspiration.

[5] Ibid, p. 399.

There are the two great phases of this subject with which we should deal in turn. These are its *process* and its *product*. Perhaps it will be better to consider the product first, because this will help us with the more difficult phase, the process.

Even though the process went on for some fifteen hundred years, it came to an end, and was therefore transient, while the product is permanent; for it is "The Word of God which liveth and abideth forever." As Jesus Himself said: "Heaven and earth shall pass away, but my words shall not pass away."

Part Two

INSPIRATION IN PRODUCT

Introduction: The best interpretation of inspiration its own.

I. THE BIBLE BEST EXAMINED IN ITS OWN LIGHT
The value of any living light.

II. WHEN THE BIBLE'S LIGHT SHINES BRIGHTEST
The three aspects of Inspiration's witness to itself.

WE COME now to *inspiration in result or product*. This phase more easily explains itself than the process, for we have the product before us. We cannot say as much for the process, as no one is now writing Scripture. The best interpretation of the Bible as an inspired book is its own, just as the best commentary on the Scriptures is the Scriptures, and the best argument for the genuineness of the Word of God is the Word itself.

I. *Chiefly because Holy Writ is a Divine Book, it is best examined in its own light.* As this is written, myriads of fireflies are flitting about in the dusk of the evening. Would that they could explain to us the marvel of their light so mysteriously produced and turned on at will! To be able to duplicate that light mechanically would be worth billions of dollars. But theirs is a living light. So also is that of Divine inspiration. It is the most valuable light that shines in this world—the Light of The Presence of God. Wherever we find this light, it is that of the Divine presence shining upon and through the human mind, soul, and personality.

44

II. To see the light of the Word of God is one thing; to have the joy of bringing it to others is another. Perhaps no one satisfactorily sees its light, who is not moved to communicate it. The "lamp unto our feet and the light unto our path" *shines brightest for us, as we use it to light the way for others.* The very genius of the Christian life is to let its light so shine, that others may see it and glorify God. So the very genius of having this light Divine is to share it, to pour out its light into other lives.

Examining the inspiration of the Word of God as a product, we shall consider its witness to itself in three aspects—the "Treasure in Earthen Vessels," that is, in Human Words; its Organizing Idea as seen from its Vital Viewpoint; and finally, a few of its Leading Themes.

IV

THE WORDS OF LIFE

Introduction: The right of Inspiration to be heard in its own interpretation.

I. THE BIBLE'S IDENTIFICATION OF THOUGHT AND WORD

Passages illustrating this. The Word of God as a message to man necessarily a record in writing. The Inspiration of the thought of Scripture and the words expressing the same considered inseparable.

II. INSPIRED THOUGHT WEDDED TO INSPIRED WORDS

No divorce of the inseparable two. Inspiration of thought alone as much a fallacy as inspiration of words alone. Verbal inspiration a misnomer. Does not say all its authors mean. The product of inspiration is both thought and word. Only the original languages inspired. Difficulties of translation.

III. SCRIPTURE WRITERS CONFESS THEY SPEAK FOR GOD, NOT FOR THEMSELVES

Great abundance of witness to this in both the Old Testament and the New.

IV. THE LANGUAGE AND TERMS BEAR WITNESS TO THE INSPIRATION OF THE HOLY SPIRIT

Instances where this is amply shown in the Scriptures. Objection considered that quotations are not *verbatim* in the New Testament from the Old Testament.

V. THE DOCTRINES OF THE CHRISTIAN FAITH REST ON THE WORDS AND THOUGHT OF SCRIPTURE

Even the form of a single word is depended upon. "It is written" used as a final court of appeal. The written statement in the Bible of the ground of salvation.

46

VI. THE CORROBORATING ATTITUDE OF SCRIPTURE
    WRITERS TO EACH OTHER
    All New Testament writers accepted the inspiration of
    those of the Old Testament. The highest testimony of all
    is that of Christ Himself.

VII. THE EVIDENCE OF INSPIRATION BY PROPHECY
    IN THE SCRIPTURES
    The mutual testimony of inspiration and prophecy. The
    inspired prophecy of Balaam. The prophetic incident of
    Moses' life when the seventy were inspired. The literal
    fulfilment of vast numbers of prophecies. Christ the Great
    Prophet.

To LET the Word of God demonstrate itself to be such,
will not be arguing in a circle. Being a Divine Message it is competent to bear witness to itself. To let
any messenger tell who he is and what he has to say,
is but fair. To let the Bible utter itself as to its inspiration is not special pleading; it is but granting
what all real jurisprudence would maintain as a right.
Now, the Bible's testimony to its inspiration is no
empty gesture. The Scriptures, however, have not
come to be tried before courts of law, but to be manifest before human hearts and consciences. "Come
now, let us reason together," saith the Word or its
Author. Persons who have tried its truths by making
their lives the result of its teaching, are sure to find
that this message of God verifies itself to be the very
product of Divine inspiration.

Holy Writ is prepared to stand or fall on *the genuineness of its Divine helpfulness*. This itself depends
upon its integrity as the very Word of God who not
only speaks through it, but stands back of all He says.
Yea more, He stands in it, for God Himself is in His

4

Word. He is in the midst of all He says, even as He is in the midst of all He does. If God is immanent in this sinful world, how much more must He dwell in His native world, the Word of His own Truth that He may come to live in all human hearts which in faith receive the Word; for "Faith cometh by hearing, and hearing by the word of God." He who is The Truth has such indissoluble union with the truth, that when God's Word is in us, He is in us too. When it is in us, it becomes part of us.

It should be a great pleasure to examine inductively this Message of God, not merely in beholding its truth, but also to find this secret of His presence come into our hearts in and by it, and in this way begin saving relation and living union with Him. Light pains diseased eyes. This is not its fault. Spiritually inflamed eyes are cured as they behold this Message of God's Presence accompanying His Word. He is no evanescent Person. His words fully represent Him in might, heart, and reliability. They do not leave us uncertain as to what He means, has for us, promises, and directs. The inspired Word shows this.

I. We may begin our discussion of the language of Scripture by noting that our *modern distinction between words and their thought is not at all in keeping with the usage of inspiration,* nor in the usage of the intervening years in the history of the Christian Church. The Bible identifies word and thought; and as a rule it uses "the word" for the thought of Scripture. Being a Message of God to man its emphasis fell on utterances, on the language as well as on the substance it expressed. For example, in His Passion Prayer our Lord said: "The words which thou gavest me, I have given unto them" (Jn. 17:8). "The words," of course, included the thought. Similar usage is, "Thy word is truth" (Jn. 17:17). "The word of God is living, and active, and sharper than any two-edged sword, piercing even to the dividing of soul and spirit, and quick (alive) to discern the thoughts and intents of the heart" (Heb. 4:12). "Making void the word of God" (Mk. 7:13). "Thou hast (the) words of eternal life" (Jn. 6:68). "Man shall not live by bread alone, but by every word that proceedeth out of the mouth of God" (Matt. 4:4). "Heaven and earth shall pass away, but my words shall not pass away" (Matt. 24:35). One might go on quoting examples of this usage indefinitely, where "the word" is so used. Over three hundred times in the Old Testament we find similar expressions—"The word of the Lord" or "of God," or "of Jehovah" or equivalent terms. "Thy word have I hid in my heart"; "The entrance of thy word giveth light"; "Thy word is true from the beginning" (Ps. 119:11, 130, 160). "My Spirit that is upon thee, and my words which I have put in thy mouth" (Isa. 59:21). To fulfil the word of Jehovah by the mouth of Jeremiah" (2 Chron. 36:21). "That the word of Jehovah by the mouth of Jeremiah might be accomplished" (Ezra 1:1). "And the Holy Spirit also beareth witness to us; for after he hath said . . ." (Heb. 10:15); then follows the quotation of Jeremiah 31:33f.

In all these and a very large number of other passages the Scriptures constantly and consistently refer
to "the word" or "the words" expressing the Divine
thought. Quite properly, then, Holy Writ speaks of
the Word of God instead of the ideas of God, and with
greater explicitness, for *the Word of God is the
Thought of God in utterance or the record thereof in
writing*. Plainly, then the inspiration of the thought is
inseparable from the inspiration of the words or language expressing it. For this reason the inspiration
of the one does not take precedence over the inspiration of the other, inasmuch as the inspiration of both
of them took place at one and the same time. Inspired
ideas do not become an inspired message until they
are embodied in inspired words.

Maudlin sentiment may profess to have "Songs
Without Words" but the Sacred Scriptures (as Paul
once called them) are such because they are written;
and to be written they must be words. We have
thoughts, but we write or speak words: we may impart our thoughts only by competent language. Dean
Burgon is quoted by H. S. Miller, M.A., as saying:

"You cannot dissect inspiration into substance and
form. As for thoughts being inspired apart from words
which give them expression, you might as well talk of a
tune without notes or a sum without figures. No such
dream can abide the daylight for a moment. It is as
illogical as it is worthless, and cannot be too sternly put
down." [1]

---

[1] *General Biblical Introduction*, p. 25. The Word-Bearer Press.

II. *Inspired thought is wedded to inspired word.*
You cannot perform a marriage if either the intended
husband or the prospective bride appear alone.   So
the inspiration of the Scriptures is the inspiration of
their thought united to inspired words.   Never is the
one found apart from the other.   Divorce the thought
from the words, or the words from the thought, and
the Scriptures have vanished.   As two are made one at
the marriage altar, so by Divine inspiration thought
and word become one.   Since inspiration is one, not
two, either thought without language, or language
without thought could not be effectually inspired.   Inspired thought without language would be abortive as
a message;   and inspired words without thought
would be meaningless.   Only when thought has passed
into the form of expression, does it become the full
product of inspiration;   and as to words without
thought, a madman could use them.   A clergyman was
asked why he did not reply to a torrent of loquacious
blasphemy.   He said, "That cannot be done, for the
poor fellow has set his mouth agoing, and gone off
and left it."   A wit has said, "She threw her mind into
neutral, but her tongue idled on."   Thought may be
found independent of words in the dumb or those to
whom language for some reason is impossible.   Persons
with the gift of language cannot think without all their
thoughts automatically shaping or embodying themselves into words spoken or unspoken.   In expressing
one's mastery of a new language, we say we are able
to think in it.   So inspiration becomes master of the

art of producing a message when its process results in the product of language appropriate and adequate.

The inspiration of thought apart from language is as much a fallacy as the inspiration of language apart from thought. The term "verbal inspiration" is a misnomer. It is misleading, for it is only half of what is meant, but not expressed by it. This incompetent expression misrepresents the faith which is as much in inspired thought as in inspired words. Apart from thought words are empty sounds, mere vacuums, nonentities. An extremist may say, "I believe that every word and every letter in the Bible is inspired." But letters cannot be inspired apart from words, and words cannot be inspired apart from the ideas they convey. Artificially separate the inspiration of the one from the other, and we create an unreality and have on our hands stark impossibility. Neither those asserting "verbal inspiration" nor those denying it are accurate, for it is only half the truth; but separated half-truths do not while apart make a whole truth. Later we shall attempt to show in the process of inspiration that every inspired writer automatically formulated with the guidance and superintendence of the Holy Spirit every thought into language, for it was *the person who was inspired,* and not merely his mind or his power of expression. Half a person, or part of him could not be inspired apart from the rest of him. That is an impossible psychology. So the product of inspiration must consist in both thought and words. We could not have the product of it in thought only. It would be a serious matter for the Divine message if both ideas and their record were not equally the product of inspiration. Half inspiration, like a person half-inspired, would be none. God's message to man came by a blessed "complicity" of united Divine and human ministry. For this reason the inspired product was infallibly recorded in human language. *The words chosen by the union of the Holy Spirit and His agents were in union with the thought expressed by them,* just as the human instruments were in union with the Spirit of God. Apart from Him these writers could not be inspired, even as apart from the Holy Spirit no thoughts could be inspired. It is essential in the Scriptures that God says what they say. Another essential is that the words uttering His message, do not misrepresent it, but are fully competent to express it. Coming from this Divine-human union the language in the original tongues is the product of complete inspiration in human words used by the Holy Spirit along with His writers.

To Divine thought human words may be found in inspired counterpart. But languages differ. It is anything but easy to translate the original languages used by inspiration without changing to some extent the original thought. Translators and translations are not necessarily inspired. When critics assume that we do not have the original text, that is a question for Textual Criticism. We believe that though the originals are gone, and only copies are to be had, the God who took care to send us His Word, has taken care to preserve its integrity in the transmission to these copies. If it be held that even the original words did not adequately express the Divine thought, where are we to look for persons in closer union with, and having greater endowment from, the Holy Spirit than the Divinely chosen writers? Many attempts to correct the Scriptures turn out in the light of archeology to be themselves in the need of correction, and not the Bible. James C. Muir's "His Truth Endureth" in recent issue shows that later archeology has rendered obsolete much Old Testament Criticism. With the archeological spade God is today marvelously corroborating the inspired pen.

Translating the original languages of the Scriptures into other tongues is not an easy matter. To find exactly corresponding words or terms is well nigh impossible in many cases. In the Authorized Version there are sheer mistranslations, as in Isaiah 9:6, "the everlasting Father" should be "the Father of eternity" or Creator of time. The Revised Version perpetuates the blunder, but puts the correct translation in the margin.

All our word-studies in both Testaments have their recognized value by assuming that the original words establish the record of what inspiration says. When translations exactly reproduce the meaning of the original text, they have the same value of the *ipsissima verba*. But paraphrases which take liberties with the original text as we have it, and break away from the original words and their sense make the passages lose much of their aptness, charm, and power; and the result is like milk with water added thereto. For example, the Revised Version translation of 2 Timothy 3 : 16 is really but a poor paraphrase having very little of "the sincere milk of the word" in it, because it takes the profound and altogether exceptional statement of inspiration about itself, and turns it into a futile truism.

III. In our endeavor to let inspiration verify itself, we may note *the confessions of the Scripture writers that they speak for God, not for themselves.* Take for example the Book of Numbers. Seventeen of its thirty-six chapters begin with, "And Jehovah said unto Moses"; and the same expression occurs thirty-seven times within these chapters. So fifty-four times is this assertion of Divine authorship repeated in this Book. All through the Old Testament there are a host of similar affirmations that it is God who is speaking. Some have taken the time and patience to count as many as two thousand instances or references to Divine authorship. Ezekiel tells when and where "the Word of Jehovah" came expressly to him. Isaiah and Jeremiah give like careful circumstantial accounts of their commission to speak for God. In Habakkuk we are told of the burden or oracle which "the prophet did see." Also in the second chapter he further says: "I will stand upon my watch, and set me upon the tower (fortress), and will look forth to see what he (Jehovah) will speak by (or with) me."

The New Testament "Confessors of the Faith" also witness most explicitly to the Divine source of what they wrote. As an example of this the Apostle John says:

"That which was from the beginning, that which we have heard, that which we have seen with our eyes, that which we beheld, and our hands handled, concerning the Word of Life (and the life was manifested, and we have seen, and bear witness, and declare unto you the life, the eternal life which was with the Father, and was manifested unto us) ; that which we have seen and heard declare we unto you" (1 Jn. 1 : 1-3).

Here we have unwearying repetition born out of overmastering conviction of the reality of the Divine manifestation to them. All the rest of the New Testament writers show the same unwavering conviction and attitude. In most cases these writers had passed through Pentecost, or had received similar post-Pentecostal enduement, and had the Holy Spirit abiding with them and resting upon them to make real to them the things of Christ. Therefore, as writers they were not strangers to the ways, workings, and movements of the Spirit of God especially in inspiration.

IV. *The very utterances or terms which these writers used bear witness to this consciousness of the Divine source of the product in writing at the behest of the Holy Spirit.* We have Paul using a very exceptional word telling how "God breathed forth" (*theopneustos*) the Scriptures. And there is Peter's Pentecostal expressoin that inspiration by the Holy Spirit w a s like the "rushing" (*pheromenes*) of a mighty wind rushing or bearing onward (*pheromenoi*) the writers of Scripture. Later these two passages will be more fully discussed. Here we may say that Peter knew by his own experience that "No prophecy ever came (was brought) by the will of man," but came "from God" (2 Peter 1 : 21). In his earlier Epistle he had written that the Old Testament prophets of the mystery of Christ's Redemption had related "by the Spirit of Christ which was in them," more than they at the time fully comprehended (1 Peter 1:11). And he went on to say, "This good tidings" (gospel) is today "preached unto you in (by) the Holy Spirit sent forth from heaven." Certainly as the same men preached by the Holy Spirit, so they wrote. In Acts 1:16 Luke refers to what "The Holy Spirit spake by the mouth of David." In First Corinthians 2:12 Paul writes, "We received, not the spirit of the world, but the Spirit which is from God; that we might know the things that were freely given to us of God." He says further: "Which things also we speak, not in words which man's wisdom teacheth." This expression, "words . . . which the Spirit teacheth," is another instance in which the identification of inspired word and thought is expressed. A direct reference to the agency of the Holy Spirit may be found in the following passage: "the mystery of Christ . . . hath now been revealed unto his holy apostles and prophets by the Spirit" (Eph. 3:5). With this may well go the word of James: "It seemed good to the Holy Spirit, and to us" (Acts 15:28). This reminds us of the word of the Lord Himself: "For it is not ye that speak, but the Spirit of your Father that speaketh in you" (Matt. 10:20). This is also mentioned in its fulfilment: "So great a salvation which having at the first been spoken through the Lord, was confirmed unto us by them that heard: God also bearing witness with them . . . by gifts of the Holy Spirit, according to his own will" (Heb. 2:3, 4). This agrees with Luke's statement: "all that Jesus began both to do and to teach . . . after that he had given commandment through the Holy Spirit unto the apostles whom he had chosen" (Acts 1:1, 2). A little later this is again referred to: "Having received of the Father the promise of the Holy Spirit, he hath poured forth this which *ye see and hear*" (Acts 2:33). And again: "We are witnesses of these things; and so is the Holy Spirit, whom he hath given to them that obey him" (Acts 5:32). Paul sharply distinguishes between the possession of the Holy Spirit and the inspiration thereof. After explaining that no commandment about the matter of virgins had been communicated to him from God, in giving his own judgment Paul significantly adds: "And I think that I also have the Spirit of God." In the closing words of Acts Luke presents what he calls "one word" by Paul: "Well spake the Holy Ghost through Isaiah the prophet unto your fathers, saying . . ." Turning to Isaiah 6:9, 10 we find the original utterance to which Paul referred, and immediately before it the story of Isaiah's call and commission. "And he (the Lord) said, Go, and tell this people." Later in 48:16 Isaiah says a remarkable thing for the Old Testament: "The Lord Jehovah hath sent me and his Spirit." The unknown author of the Epistle to the Hebrews, quoting Jeremiah 31:33, 34 says: "And the Holy Spirit also beareth witness to us" (Heb. 10:15). This means that the Holy Spirit spake through both Jeremiah and "us." We find Matthew also acknowledging the inspiration of the 110th

Psalm: "How then doth David in the Spirit call him Lord?" (Matt. 22:43). Referring to the same utterance Mark says: "David himself said in the Holy Spirit" (12:36). The account in 2 Samuel 23:1, 2 quotes David as saying: "The Spirit of Jehovah spake by me, and his word was upon my tongue." These passages chosen here and there throughout the Scriptures are but a small fraction of the number of witnesses and evidences which may be adduced to show the Divine authorship of Holy Writ by the Holy Spirit.

In opposition to the inspiration of the Scriptures in word as well as in thought it has been argued that the frequent quotations in the New Testament not in the exact words of the Old Testament show that the words of the Scriptures do not share in their inspiration. The fatal assumption here is that inspiration could not give a summary instead of *verbatim* reproduction of the said passages. The objectors would have to be able to show that it was always the Holy Spirit's intention to quote the whole passage word for word, instead of using a summary of its meaning applying to the matter in point. Then too allowance should be made for the constant change in forms and modes of expression in which words even reverse their meaning. In exact verbal quotation of "He that letteth will let," the explanation would have to go along that it means, "He that hindereth will hinder." In no case did New Testament quotations from the Old Testament do violence to the meaning or truth in the latter.

V. *The great doctrines of the Christian Faith are grounded in the record of the Scriptures.* Faith in the very words of inspiration is such that important teaching about the Lord Himself is based on the form of a single word. An example of this is Galatians 3 : 16, "He saith not, And to seeds, as of many; but as of one, And to thy seed, which is Christ" (Gen. 22 : 18; Rom. 9 : 7; John 8 : 37, 39). So closely are the Scriptures identified with God, they are personified and made to speak, exhibit, and foresee as though they were God Himself. "For the scriptures saith unto Pharaoh, even for this purpose have I raised thee up, that I might show my power in thee, that my name might be declared throughout all the earth" (Rom. 9 : 17). "And the scriptures foreseeing that God would justify the heathen" (Gal. 3 : 8). We behold this exceedingly high regard for Holy Writ in that therein it is called *"The Oracles of God."* This expression means not merely words reported for Him, but the very words which proceeded out of the mouth of God. "Chiefly because unto them were committed (entrusted) the oracles of God" (Rom. 3 : 2; also Heb. 5 : 12; Acts 7 : 38; 1 Peter 4 : 11). Those who have fully recognized the Scriptures as the inspired Word of God, have therefore used them as a final court of appeal, settling what God had said or willed. Because of this the authoritative phrase was, "It is written." Even Satan used this expression in tempting our Lord, when our Saviour replied to him, "Again it is written."

The reliability of the Bible as the inspired Word of God leads to acceptance of it as the *great authority on what is the Divine ground of salvation.* "These things have I written unto you, that ye may know that ye have eternal life, even unto you that believe on the name of the Son of God" (1 Jn. 5:13). "So faith cometh of hearing, and hearing of the word of Christ" (Rom. 10:17). The means of salvation is well explained in the Word. Paul says: "For I delivered unto you first of all that which I also received, how that Christ died for our sins according to the scriptures; and that he was buried, and that he rose again the third day according to the scriptures" (1 Cor. 15: 3, 4; also 1 Thes. 2:13). "The exceeding great and precious promises," of which Peter speaks (1 Peter 1:4) as coming from the knowledge of Christ are also the means of knowing God by faith. It is said that the Bible contains thirty thousand promises. One promise of God is as valid and dependable as any or all of them, because of the reliability of Him who gave them, "For he is faithful that promised" (Heb. 10:23).

VI. *A corroboration of inspiration, which might be called a sidewise one, is the attitude of the Scripture writers to one another.* Had the New Testament writers attacked the inspiration of the Old Testament writings, both could not have been inspired of God. What do we find? Peter says: "The prophets . . . searching what time or what manner of time the Spirit of Christ which was in them did point unto, when it testified beforehand the sufferings of Christ, and the glories that should follow them. To whom it was re-

vealed, that not unto themselves, but unto you, did they
minister these things, which now have been announced
unto you through them that brought good tidings unto
you by the Holy Spirit sent forth from heaven; which
things the angels desire to look into" (1 Peter 1: 11,
12). "God having of old time spoken unto the fathers
in the prophets . . . hath at the end of these days
spoken unto us in a Son" (Heb. 1: 1, 2). "Now all
this is come to pass, that it might be fulfilled which was
spoken by the Lord through the prophet" (Matt. 1:
22; also 2: 15). By inference Peter classes Paul's
epistles as Scripture (2 Peter 3: 16). And Paul
quotes from Luke as Scripture (1 Tim. 5: 18). Here
Paul couples, "The laborer is worthy of his hire"
(Lu. 10: 7), with Deuteronomy 25: 4.

Manifestly the confident consciousness of the writers having the mind of Christ carried *authority* with it.
Paul says: "Who hath known the mind of the Lord,
that he should instruct him? But we have the mind
of Christ" (1 Cor. 2: 16). Also he says, "The Gospel
which was preached by me, that is not after man. For
neither did I receive it from man, nor was I taught
it, but it came to me by revelation of Jesus Christ"
(Gal. 1: 11, 12; also 2 Thes. 2: 15; 3: 6, 14).

In seeking to let inspiration bear testimony to itself,
only a small fraction of it is here used, for the whole
Bible would have to be quoted to give it all. There is,
however, reserved the highest rank of testimony for
the last—that of Christ Himself. Of course, we are
here compelled to depend upon the inspired record to
furnish us with what the Master said about the Scrip-

tures. If He had this faith in inspiration, so may we. He had confidence enough in the very words and terms of Holy Writ to use them in defense of His claim to be the Son of God. First let us note that He says: "Ye search the scriptures, because ye think that in them ye have eternal life; and these are they which bear witness of me" (Jn. 5:39). Next we note the instance in which He silenced the Pharisees: "He saith unto them, How then doth David in the Spirit call him Lord? . . . If David then calleth him Lord, how is he his Son? (Matt. 22:43, 45). He then offered finally the direct defense of His Deity: "If he called them gods, unto whom the word of God came *(and the scripture cannot be broken),* say ye of him whom the Father hath sanctified and sent into the world, Thou blasphemest, because I said, I am the Son of God? (Jn. 10:35, 36). Here are two things all-important: the inspired, unbreakable Scriptures, and the Deity of Him who said so. Either may be taken as corroboration of the other.

VII. *The Evidence for Inspiration furnished by Prophecy in the Scriptures.* Inspiration undoubtedly bears testimony to prophecy, even as prophecy testifies for inspiration. There are two senses in which the word prophecy is used in the Bible, the general sense of "speaking forth," and the special one of "predicting in God's name." The first is the usual sense and really includes the second. The predictive order of prophecy is meant when we say: Read the Word of God to be up with the times, and its prophecies to be

5

ahead of the times. Those who believe these inspired predictions of the Bible expect the greatest things from God. Christ Himself explained that doubt and darkness had come to the disciples because "slow of heart to believe in all that the prophets had spoken" (Lu. 24: 25). This specifically referred to our Lord's death.

There are scores of Biblical prophecies which have been fulfilled to the letter. Only two of the prophets may be mentioned here who were contemporaries— Balaam and Moses. The first prophet seems to have come almost out of nowhere. He was an unreliable character who was hired by fearful enemies of Israel to curse them, but was held back by the direct prevention of God, and made to bless and prophesy great things for them and even for the coming Messiah. "I see him, but not now; I behold him, but not nigh: There shall come forth a star out of Jacob, and a sceptre shall· rise out of Israel" (Num. 24: 17). Strange that so perverse a prophet could be so used of God. He said: "Must I not take heed to speak that which Jehovah putteth in my mouth?" (Num. 23: 12). He was a low order of prophet put to death by Israel because of an insidious evil he wrought against them. (Josh. 13: 22; Jude 11). Vastly superior to Balaam, Moses was equally law-giver and prophet, and marvellously endued by the Holy Spirit had a familiarity with God that would have exalted in pride and self-importance a lesser man. On the contrary Moses was greatly humbled by these greatest of exaltations. This is shown by a beautiful incident in his life, and concerning prophecy specially it shows his magnanimous humility and self-forgetfulness. The account is as follows: "And Jehovah said unto Moses, Gather unto me seventy men of the elders of Israel . . . and I will come down and talk with thee there: and I will take of the Spirit which is upon thee, and will put it upon them; and they shall bear the burden of the people with thee, that thou bear it not thyself alone. . . . And it came to pass, that, when the Spirit rested upon them, they prophesied, but they did so no more." But the Spirit rested on two young men who began to prophesy in the camp. Joshua asked Moses to forbid them. "And Moses said unto him, Art thou jealous for my sake? would that all Jehovah's people were prophets, that Jehovah would put his Spirit upon them!" (Num. 11:16-29). Perhaps no human being bore such heavy burdens as did this great man of God; but he remained to the end the unspoiled spokesman for God.

The very numerous and marvellous prophesies in the Old Testament and in the New also which have been fulfilled to the letter are sufficient attestation to the inspiration which gave them. They were not uncertain statements; but were recorded in the specific words which are with us to this day. Chiefest among all the prophets is He who is our Prophet, Priest, and King, or our Revealer, Redeemer, and Ruler. "God having of old time spoken unto the fathers in the prophets by divers portions and in divers manners, hath at the end of these days spoken unto us in his Son" (Heb. 1:1, 2). The prophecy of the Apocalypse opens with the acknowledgment that this is "The Revelation of

Jesus Christ, which God gave him to show unto his servants, even the things which must shortly come to pass: and he sent and signified it by his angel unto his servant John, who bare witness of the word of God, and of the testimony of Jesus Christ, even of all the things that he saw. Blessed is he that readeth, and they that hear the words of the prophecy, and keep the things that are written therein: for the time is at hand." How like to this are the words which fell from the blessed lips of the Master during his days on earth: "Blessed are they that hear the word of God, and keep it" (Lu. 11:28).

V

VIEWPOINT AND ORGANIZING IDEA

Introduction: Right Relation unto God is the Bible's viewpoint, and Redemption unto Life Eternal is its organizing idea.

I. KIND OF SPIRIT ORIGINATES TYPE OF THOUGHT, ORGANIZES ITS MATERIAL, AND DETERMINES THE CHARACTER OF THINKING
God's viewpoint rules in all the Scriptures. Man created in adaptation to Right Relation to God. This lost, Redemption became the organizing idea of the Message of God to man. Man a citizen of two worlds. The Bible recognizes this world the battlefield with the Evil One.

II. THE SCRIPTURES REVEAL GOD AS PERSONAL
The personal defined as the highest conceivable type of life. Self-determination essential in personal realization. It may lead to spiritual suicide. Sin results in loss of capacity for God and of affinity with Him.

III. ABANDONMENT OF RIGHT RELATION TO GOD MEANS CESSATION OF RIGHT PERSONAL BE-COMING OR REVERSAL OF LIFE-MOVEMENT
Selfishness as a viewpoint of human existence. The Scriptures a Book of man's Justification or the Word of Condemnation according to whether he has become a Christ-created personality or not. The offer of Eternal Life the central fact of Divine Revelation. The Bible's estimate of the seriousness of sin.

IN STUDYING the product of inspiration we find that the viewpoint of the Scriptures is *Right Relation to God;* and as seen from it their organizing idea is *Redemption unto Life Eternal.* The Word of God is most appropriately written from His standpoint. In this it is unique, for it is the only book in the world so written. As Sir Walter Scott said: "There is but One Book."

I. *Everywhere kind of spirit originates type of thought, organizes its material, and determines the character of thinking.* The greater the spirit producing it, the greater must be the book it sends forth. As the Spirit of Life Eternal, the Holy Spirit has inspired all the material of the Bible, and organized all its contents true to its great point of view—Right Relation to God. This is perhaps the main reason why the Scriptures are so wondrous a unity—God's viewpoint rules throughout them. This is why Holy Writ has one organific idea from its opening words, "In the beginning God," to its close in prayer to God the Son, "Come quickly."

When God created man in His own image and likeness, He constituted his personality in adaptation to right relation to Himself. But sin blurred that image and debased that likeness. Man's first experience of spiritual life in right relation to God was short-lived. This necessitated the provision of the permanent type of religious life. The Law need not be mistaken for this. So Redemption unto Life Eternal became the organizing idea of the Bible, because re-creation in the image and likeness of the Son was God's "Plan of Salvation." Then the whole difference between abiding in spiritual death and escaping into everlasting life lies in whether man accepts or refuses the new relation to God in Jesus Christ. In receiving the Son of God as Saviour man takes Him for his counterpart

environment of Life Eternal. In this way God becomes the end and fulfilment of human existence.

Being created body, soul, and spirit man was constituted a citizen of two worlds. As the Word of
God reveals, not all the realm of spirit is in harmony
with God. There is correspondence with an evil order
of supernatural spirit, the Bible says, which for man
is reciprocity with an environment of spiritual death.
Union with this enemy of God and man can have but
one result—that of ending right relation to God. While
naturalism and its modern theologies have bowed the
devil out of existence, his havoc in human life all the
more goes on in a way adequately and accurately de-
scribed only by the term "diabolical." Here we may
note the wisdom of the Word and the power of the
Redemption it proclaims, that Christ is able to, and
does spoil Satan's power over man. To this end He
both died and rose again, "That through death he
might bring to naught him that hath the power of
death, that is, the devil" (Heb. 2: 14).

II. *The Holy Scriptures reveal God as Personal*
and religion as personal relation to Him. This is the
highest order or type of life of which we are able to
conceive whether in God or in man. While Divine
Personality is the absolute fulness and perfection of
character and being, man is created an order of highest
possible personal becoming. Governing this possibility
is his power of self-determination and self-realization.
In this way he chooses the goal of his immortal existence. So his personal becoming is either in likeness

or in unlikeness to God by either alliance with Him or
by turning away from Him.   Which is chosen now
depends upon whether or not man lives, moves, and has
his affinity with God's bestowal of Himself in the
Redeemer.   No matter what the insanity of sin may
call it, for man to turn from God in Christ is spiritual
suicide.   The Gospel as well as the Law so reveal it.
For man to deny God His rightful place, is to violate
his own as well as God's nature.   Every atom of man's
nature is mortally damaged by the disruption of right
personal relation with his Maker.   And because of
man's immortality such abandonment of right relation
with God opens up an eternity and infinity of evil results which are infallibly registered and organized in
human personality.   For man all well-being is absolutely inseparable from right relationship to God.   To
break continuity of the activity of right relation with
Him is immediately to develop unfitness for communion with Him.   Then in the process of man's personal
becoming he loses priceless capacity for God and that
blessed fellowship with Him which comes by living
with and for Him.

III.   From God's point of view, which the Scriptures always take, there is made emphatically plain and
undeniably clear, that *abandonment of right relation
to God is the cessation of right personal becoming, for
it is the reversal of trend or direction of life-movement.*
When self and selfishness displaces God, it becomes
the viewpoint of human existence.   When man has
turned his back upon God, his selfishness wanders in

barren wastes, seeking rest and finding none. Then the Bible becomes the most difficult of books to read and enjoy, for in it from first to last the sinner is compelled to face God. This is the remarkable thing about Holy Writ: *every page brings us face to face with God*. Its inspiration causes the Eyes of Omniscience to look upon us and within us at every sentence of these Oracles of God. Blessed be God! the same Word of God also reveals His blessed invitation and promise that there is remission of sins.

Because of the nature of their Viewpoint and Organific Idea, the Scriptures must to be to us either a Book of Condemnation or the Word of Justification. John says: "And this is the witness that God gave unto us eternal life, and this life is in his Son" (1 Jn. 5: 11). This record or witness is the very warp and woof of the message of the Word. This is its fundamental revelation and controlling conception which organizes all the material of the Scriptures about itself. Not in the New Testament only, but in the Old Testament as well—Law, Sacrifices, Hebrew History, and Prophecy lead up to the greatest event in all eternity, the giving of Christ as the means of man's everlasting Redemption. As Philip said: "We have found him of whom Moses in the law, and the prophets, wrote, Jesus of Nazareth" (Jn. 1: 45).

Another thing which Holy Writ makes perfectly clear, is that we are not saved from the law but from its condemnation, even unto the law of the spirit of life in Christ Jesus. The Levitical candle-sacrifices lit the way until "the Sun of Righteousness arose with healing in his wings." These foregleams before the great sacrifice in Christ served to educate appreciation of sacrifice. The Gospel story further explains that only a re-begetting of human personality by the Incorruptible Seed of Life Eternal could integrate the substance and organize the activity of this life in man; and thereby bring forth the new order of Christ-created personality, victorious over sin, and having the unsearchable riches of the life of the Godhead mediated in unity, love, fellowship, and sacrificial fulfilment poured into the mould of the new man in Christ.

One of the Great Outstanding Revelations of the Word of God is *The Seriousness of Sin.* By the Holy Spirit's inspiration Paul tells how "sin is shown to be sin" (Rom. 7:13) by its use or misuse of that which is good, "By working death to me by that which is good." The most terrible arraignment of sin to be found anywhere is in the first of Romans. Perhaps Paul also in the sixth, seventh and eighth chapters of Romans, and John in both Gospel and Epistle sound the deepest depths in explanation of the sinfulness of sin. How shallow is any attempted profundity which makes light of sin. "Fools make a mock at sin" (Prov. 13:9). To be a fool spiritually in such matters is much worse than to be a mere mental fool, for the latter is not responsible. If we refuse what God says in His Word about iniquity, it does not matter where else we seem to agree with Him. All true understanding and agreement with God must begin in heeding His estimate of our own sin. "Against thee, even thee, have I sinned, and done that which is evil in thy sight"

(Ps. 51:4). Here David shows himself to be really "a man after God's own heart" in taking sides with God against himself and his sin. This results from the work of the Holy Spirit within. Jesus said: "And he (the Comforter, Advocate, or Paraclete) when he is come, will convict the world in respect of sin" (Jn. 16:8). The next verse says, "Of sin, because they believe not on me."

The sinfulness of sin is the counterpart doctrine which makes possible the realization of the Greatness of Divine Redemption. Wherever or whenever it happened, sin began and has continued by substituting something other than God as the means of personal becoming and fulfilment. This is sin's substitutionary theory of satisfaction. But it brings forth death instead: "Then the lust, when it hath conceived, beareth sin; and sin, when it is fullgrown, bringeth forth death" (Jas. 1:15). Man by his personal and God-given power of self-determination may turn against God, and not only refuse Him, but realize himself in enmity to God. "For the mind of the flesh is death, . . . because the mind of the flesh is enmity against God: for it is not subject to the law of God, neither indeed can it be: and they that are in the flesh cannot please God" (Rom. 8:6-8). Thus the soul of sin is an order of personal realization in antipathy to God, self-realization in faithlessness to Him, of distrust in Him, of unbelief toward Him, of hate for Him instead of love, of aversion to Him instead of finding Him the Supreme Attraction. Sin is sodden selfishness instead of making God the Supreme Interest in life.

The process of sin is its personalization. There is no sin except by or within persons. The awful thing about iniquity is that once beginning, there is no end to the possibility of its multiplication. As the Welsh proverb says, "One sin draws a hundred after it." The growth of sin is the growth of personality in unlikeness to God, the increase of unfitness for correspondence with Him. There is a growth in spiritual death, until the last atom of nature which may respond to God is gone and full personalization of anti-God nature, spirit and development is reached. Then there is nothing left to which God may appeal in love and sacrifice. The soul being set on fire of hell has perpetual burning, consuming within the last remnants of personality belonging to God. Sin is the architect and builder of the bottomless pit. It is that hate of, and flight from God that finally plunges downward into the emptiness and blackness of darkness of an eternal nowhere. Eternal punishment is for eternal sinning. Having lost God out of itself, personality can realize itself only in an everlasting negation to God. All its satisfaction and achievement is then in destruction, dissolution, and desolation, within and without. "Know ye not, that to whom ye present yourselves as servants unto obedience, his servants ye are whom ye obey; whether of sin unto death or of obedience unto righteousness?" (Rom. 6:16). This agrees with what Jesus Himself said, "Verily, verily I say unto you,

Every one that committeth sin is the bondservant of sin" (Jn. 8:34).

From all this it seems that Redemption is *from* vastly more and *to* vastly more than we are now able fully to comprehend. To put out the fires of hell within, to redeem personality from spiritual death requires a new life, a new nature, a new order of self-realization, and the new means of self-fulfilment, namely, God in Christ. Sin may still hover on the outskirts of life on earth, but Life Eternal all the more hating it for this, is bound for final and absolute deliverance from it through union with Christ and being in Him forever. For the present, one measure of oneness with the Lord is the height of our horror of iniquity. It was a superb saint, the chief of saints, who counted himself "the chief of sinners." He was really the chief of successful servants in the Ministry of Christ.

VI

SOME LEADING THEMES OF HOLY WRIT

I. THE TRIUNE GODHEAD
The doctrine of the Trinity compelled by the Incarnation. God the greatest theme of the Bible. Offices of the Persons of the Godhead. Historical summary of the Trinity seeking after man to redeem him.

II. THE BIBLE'S STORY OF MAN'S REDEMPTION
The Old Testament's provisional remedy for sin. Atonement replaced by Divine Redemption. Two main types of interpretation of Redemption. The eternal sacrificial relation of the Trinity in itself. Holiness reaches its highest manifestation in the sacrificial. The blotting out of sin strategic in Redemption. Life in Christ. The solution of sin's problem in human self-realization in Christ.

III. THE MINISTRY OF THE HOLY SPIRIT
Personal characteristics of the Holy Spirit revealed in His Ministry. He is the means of all communion with God. The Bible the Great Textbook on Prayer. The Holy Spirit the Author of Holy Writ. His threefold Ministry in relation to the Father, the Son, and the Christian life.

IV. THE PRESENCE OF GOD
The various forms of manifestations of God's Presence in Old Testament days. Christ is Immanuel, God with us. Sin's Effect on the Sense of God's Presence. The Remedy.

V. THE WILL OF GOD IN THE CHRISTIAN LIFE
The life-long Campaign against Evil. Two forms of God's Will in relation to us. The more Symmetry of Personality, the less struggle to do God's will. The Bible the Daily Journal of living the Will of our Lord and Master.

VI. THE WORD OF GOD THE BREAD OF EVERLASTING LIFE
The correspondence of Life and Food. The Bread of Greatness. The Word in Personal relation to God. A Mind preëmpted by Biblical Truth.

VII. THE BIBLE THE BOOK OF DIVINE FULFILMENT
1. It reveals the Divine Nature as always True to Itself.
2. God Fulfilling Himself in all His relations, in the Trinity and Elsewhere.
3. All Redemption's Fulfilment reaches back to the Divine Sovereignty.
4. God Fulfilling Himself in all His Activities. God's Daring to Create Personality.
5. Eternal life lived in the eternal spirit of the Sacrifice of Christ.
6. The Divine Fulfilment in Love and Sacrifice. The Fulfilment of His Followers.
7. The Great Fulfilment of the Godhead in Unity. This Tested at Calvary. The Scriptures' Testimony to the Unity of the Trinity during the Death of Christ. The Throne of God and of the Lamb.

THE Scriptures neglect none of the great themes of the Christian life. In the preceding chapter we have touched upon, Right Relation to God, Redemption unto Life Eternal, and the Seriousness of Sin. Here there is not space to survey all the other great themes, nor can we do more than touch upon the seven subjects considered in this chapter.

No doubt God is the greatest among the themes of the Bible. In the Old Testament He is Jehovah, the Personal God. Due to His manifestation in God the Son we have in the New Testament the tri-personal Godhead—The Father, the Son, and the Holy Spirit. The coming of the Christ compelled the doctrine of the Trinity. He revealed the Father as God over us, the Son as God for us, and the Holy Spirit as God in us. This is fragmentary and does not emphasize the Divine Tri-unity. It will be considered last in this chapter.

I. THE TRIUNE GODHEAD

Each Person in the Triune Godhead has a Trinity of Offices. Those of the Father are Authority, Purpose or Plan, and Source. The Son's are, Revelation, Creation, and Sacrifice in Person. The Holy Spirit's are, Impartation, Fellowship, and Fulfilment. This means that the Father is Ultimate Source and Sovereign; but each Divine Person is Lord in the realm of His own functions. The Son is the Agent of Creation and the very substance of Divine Revelation, "God manifest in the flesh." As Sacrifice in Person He became Incarnate that He might become Redemption's Sacrifice in Person. "But now once at the end of the ages hath he been manifested to put away sin by the sacrifice of himself" (Heb. 9:26). By the Holy Spirit all Divine communication, impartation, fellowship and consummation are effectually realized.

The Scriptures relate the story of man's creation quickly followed by his forsaking God, and the Divine age-long effort to remedy the disaster. The Old Testament recounts the patient providences of God until in the fulness of time the Supreme Providence in Christ appeared. The Law, the Prophets, and the Hagiographa tell of the supplementary ways in which God sought man to reach and bless him. Then in the New Testament came the Crowning Manifestation of God in Christ's Enhumanation followed by His Life Ministry, Crucifixion, Resurrection, Ascension, and Enthronement. God also manifested Himself in the Holy Spirit by Pentecostal origination of the Church

as an evangelizing instrument. In it as an organism
the authority of Christ was continued, but not so much
in it as an organization. The greatest exploitation in
all the ages may be found there.

II. THE BIBLE STORY OF MAN'S REDEMPTION

In the Old Testament "Atonement" is the great word
for temporary and provisional remedy for iniquity.
In the New Testament the word does not appear at
all. The Holy Spirit had a reason for replacing it with
Redemption, Propitiation, Reconciliation, and Sacrifice. Who Christ is and what He became by His sacrificial death must ever be foundational to the meaning and merit of His Redemption. His own challenge
to the Jews was, "What think ye of the Christ? Whose
son is he?" (Matt. 22:42). There are two main types
in interpretation of Divine Redemption. One kind
centers in law, penalty, eternal Divine suffering, the
majesty of God, the price of ransom, and many other
such considerations. The other type centers in the
Person of Christ, what He became to God and man
by His obedience unto death, what He realized in His
Person by sacrificial fulfilment of the will of God,
and what He was enabled to give to man through His
death and resurrection. Nowhere does the Scripture
say that He propitiated God by His death and suffering. Rather it says, "He is the propitiation for our
sins" (1 Jn. 2:2; 4:10; Rom. 3:25), for He is the
only means to blot them out. Nothing could ever allay
God's indignation with sin but its extermination. If
iniquity still controlled the making of human person-

6

ality, went on shaping men into co-workers with Satan, Christ might have died a thousand times and God be as angry as ever with sin. Nothing could ever be done to make sin less damnable to God. Christ became that propitiation because He perfectly fulfilled the sacrificial nature of God in surrendering Himself to the process in which His Person was riven to pour out His life, His blood which is the only thing in the history of eternity that can blot out sin. And His wounds remain unhealed until the last soul is saved. Never was the righteousness of God more manifest than in providing the efficacy to end the unrighteousness of the existence of sin.

The great problem of Redemption was to redeem man unto God, unto life in Him. There is only one damnation that befits sin, that is, to end it and its power of demonizing humanity. There is but one way of escaping from God's vengeance on our sin, and that is to run to Him by way of Christ, the sacrifice for us. This not only restores the God-loving, sin-hating nature to us, but provides the very life that is in Christ to be our life also. Faith in Him puts us within the New Covenant with God that He is. Faith in God in Christ is foundational to all personal relation to Him. Fighting the good fight of faith means maintaining faith in the God of Redemption at all cost.

Redemption is the reëstablishment of life in God as well as of right relation to Him. As God is the center and circumference of the Scriptures, so Christ is the center and substance of our redemption unto life eternal. He is the beginning and the end of the Christian life. He is "the Lord our righteousness." He is our New Covenant with God. We enter into this covenant by faith in Him, and there find by the same faith the sure standing of acceptance with God and legal justification. He who "was obedient unto death," became the death of spiritual death and the life of the redeemed forever. Redemption, to be such, is unto life eternal.

The strategic thing, the fundamental purpose God set out to secure in Redemption was the blotting out of sin and sinning. Nothing that ever could be done, could change God's feeling and attitude to sin. Any sacrifice that left sin free to control the self-determination and personal realization of man would be useless. Christ's death on the Cross could not make sin one whit more agreeable to God. If possible, it must have made Him hate and abhor it all the more.

Human personality to be truly redeemed must have life in Christ, personal realization in and by Him, become what He is in moral character and spiritual affinity through union with Him. A sin-proof soul is one in indestructible union with Christ. Personality in man is so like what it is in God, Divine self-respect must respect its integrity to the full. Redemption of human personality cannot be compelled by almighty power or even by absolute will. It is the self-giving love of Christ that constrains us, the self-sacrifice of Christ that compels our hearts in response, and draws us to God through His sacrifice for us. Infinitely great and important as salvation is, it cannot be foisted upon man. From beginning to end the Bible shows that man must either choose or refuse to accept salvation by God. That power of spiritual selection lies at the very beginning of and continues through all life, and especially in Redemption-life. So the Scriptures all the way through represent God as appealing to man to come unto Him, that He may do for man all that he needs, for God can do everything for man except accept for him the gift which God offers to him.

The history of man's straying from God into inexcusable unrighteousness, and also how the sacrificial love of God followed after the sinner, is the worst of all tragedies turned into the sweetest story ever told. This is as true for the individual as for the race; for every saved person has his own story of straying, and of God's pursuit, solicitation, and recovery. This story of Divine Redemption passes comparison, for it is "the love of Christ passing knowledge."

In the Scriptures God in Christ is faithfully set forth as the one and only solution of the infinitely deep problem of sin solved by right relation to Him, right living for Him, and right realization in human personality. In this life we shall never fully understand how deep has been the personal cost to God, how far down He had to go in sacrifice to get under man in sin and sin in man to establish him in righteousness of life and character. Nor can we now measure how far up we shall yet go with Christ, when He shall come again to share with us His glory for ever.

III. THE MINISTRY OF THE HOLY SPIRIT

As we find the main features of Christ's Person, Nature, and Saving Power in His Great Work of

Redemption, so do we discover the Personality and chief characteristics of the Nature of the Holy Spirit revealed in His Ministry. As a rule the Holy Spirit does not witness of Himself. He cannot, for example, become the Author of the Holy Scriptures without manifesting Himself therein and thereby. It is therefore His great task to produce Holiness. As the Work reveals the Workman, so the inspiration of Holy Writ makes known what kind of a spirit the Holy Spirit is. He is always going forth from the Father and the Son, always giving, imparting, or communicating.

The Holy Spirit is also the Source and Helper in all communion with God. All true prayer is inspired by the Spirit of God. The Bible is the great Textbook on prayer. It teaches the necessity, the continuity, and the art of prevailing prayer. But for the Holy Spirit no human person would ever pray to God in reality. And His prayer in us is always accompanied by His prayer for us, "For we know not how to pray as we ought; but the Spirit Himself maketh intercession for us with groanings which cannot be uttered; and He that searcheth the hearts knoweth what is the mind of the Spirit, because he maketh intercession for the saints according to the will of God" (Rom. 8: 26, 27).

As already said more than once, the Holy Spirit is the Divine Agent of inspiration of the Scriptures. He is also the secret of their marvellous unity, and of their being a living Book. He it was who "was brooding" or "hovering upon the face of the waters" in creation. Somewhat in the same way He brooded into being the

Bible. In the Old Testament He is known at first simply as the power of God at work in the world, the instrumental contact of the Divine with the natural. He was also God imparting the breath of life in man's making. He is the Inspirer of all God's workmen. When the fulness of time was come, He acted as the Divine Engendering Agent in the Incarnation to bring forth in the world God's Great Redemptive Worker. No doubt He was active in supporting the Son of God when He was being tortured to death. After the Resurrection He has imparted Christ to as many as became Children of God by Him. Since the Ascension He has been the "Other Paraclete," representing Christ on earth throughout this age and till He comes again.

The Holy Spirit is the Divine Person who manifests the attitude and reaction of God in contact with human life. He is the sensitivity of God in touch with man. Because the Book of books is the Word of the living God, attitude to it is attitude to the Holy Spirit. So it is the Spirit who is "grieved," "quenched," and "resisted." His ministry is in touch with the Christian life from beginning to end. He it is who enables us to enter into fellowship with God, to get great things from Him, and to fulfil ourselves in Him. The Spirit is the Great Witness for God and to God. Because of His Authorship the Bible is the greatest witness for God among books. He is the Witness of God who witnesses with our spirits that we are the children of God; and His witness is truth.

So to speak, the Holy Spirit creates the atmosphere of God. No soul can live in or with God without the

Spirit, for He is the Spirit of all life in God. So He is the impartation of life for and of Christ to every son of God. He is the Spirit of Christ in Revelation and Redemption. He is the Spirit of Love, of Grace, of Sacrifice, of Life, of Truth, of Power, and of Holiness. He is the Omnipresence of God which may become His Immanence; and He is the Immanence which makes possible Union with Christ and Obedience to the Father. He makes way in our hearts for the Father and the Son, makes them the reality they are to us. He is the *Efficiency* of God in Redemption even as Christ is the *Efficacy*.

IV. THE PRESENCE OF GOD

The Bible being the topmost textbook on the Presence of God, most surely the Divine Presence must be one of its great themes. Since the Spirit and the Word of God are here, we may be sure God Himself is here, for by His Omnipresence we have the guarantee that He can never be an absentee Deity.

In the Old Testament He manifested His Presencee in various ways—in theophanies, the Pillar of Cloud and of Fire, the Angel of His Presence (lit., of His face), and in many other forms. In the New Testament Immanuel (God with us) came to us. Man may forsake God; but God never forsakes him. Even loss of the sense of His Presence, or of right regard for Him does not cause Him to depart. So often does it happen as it did with Jacob, "God was in this place, and I knew it not." But the Most High is as truly with our departed friends as He is with us. The One

Hundred and Thirty-ninth Psalm beautifully teaches that, go where we may, He is the ever present God, for "Thou art there."

The Scriptures teach the divine art of adjustment to the Presence of God. Prayer, for example, is not wrestling with God's unwillingness or "reluctance," as Bishop Brooks says, but taking hold of His Presence, His willing, helping outreach. The Scriptures are able to educate us in sane sensibility and proper response to the Presence of God. For this reason Holy Writ is the greatest Book of devotional help in "Practicing the Presence of God." The Sacred Word reveals that the inner strength of our lives as well as the outer manifestation lies in their communion or correspondence with the very Presence of God.

The Bible is not silent upon the effect of sin, the way it weakens our sense of God's Presence and lessens our power to lay hold upon it. We would have been still walking with God in Gardens of Fellowship, had not our iniquity cast us out. Then, too, the realization of the Divine Presence is the law of power for service. While there is no absentee God, alas, there are hosts of absentee Christians, having left the Father to wander and wallow in prodigal wastes, as told in the Parable of the Lost Son.

The Word teaches that maintained filial relation enjoying fellowship with the Father through the Son and the Holy Spirit is the primal means of maintained spiritual strength, for "to be weak is to be miserable," and "in the presence of God is fulness of joy forever." There is also unequalled protection in the Divine Pres-

ence, and steadfast assurance both for this life and
and for the world to come. The Bible would train us
so to live in the Presence of God here, that we become
adequately fitted for, and adapted to, the greater manifestation of the immediate Presence of God hereafter.

V. THE WILL OF GOD IN THE CHRISTIAN LIFE

The Scriptures reveal the nature of the conflict of
the Christian life with its enemies who are also the foes
of God.   In Old Testament days the struggle was
much the same in the nature of the campaign; but the
weapons of their warfare were far from being as
efficient as ours. God fully knows the processes and
struggles necessary to produce the kind of personality
He desires, and He gives us in His Word most valuable information about all this.   When the evil of this
world is certain not to leave us alone, we must know
how to recognize, meet, and master it. The Word of
Life teaches us how the "Holy War" may be won.

It is not just one fight, two or three battles, but a
life-long campaign in this conflict with evil. The Bible
makes clear what the issue is, the strength, persistence,
and tactics of the enemy, our own weaknesses and
where our strength lies, the armor of offense and of
defense, the sword of the Spirit which is the Word of
God, and who the Captain of our salvation is. If it is
the will of God that we must fight to win, it is also the
will of God that we must suffer to succeed.

There is the will of God what to do, and also the
will of God what to receive and submit to. The Bible
reveals the ways and workings of God's nature, and

makes clear the law of His sovereign nature in relation to us. The Sovereignty of God is one of the very
great features of this Divine relation. Within the
Trinity it is a form of fellowship. There cannot be
full faith in His will on our part without counterpart
understanding. Credulity cannot please God. Blind,
ignorant faith may easily forsake Him. The Word is
not only God's will concerning us in all fulness and
sufficiency; it also explains the Divine Sovereignty in
its reasonableness, wisdom, and profit.

On the other hand the Scriptures reveal us to ourselves, the deceitfulness of the sinful human heart, the
necessity and the way of changing it. "Out of the heart
are the issues of life." If it is dead to the will of God,
only death can come from it, for "the natural man is
at enmity with God." If the heart is alive with love
to God, a life of love to Him shall issue from it. In
full rounded development we become the more sym-
metrical, and the less will be the strain and struggle to
accept the will of God in everything. Love by faith
may produce submission sane and strong enough to
kiss the rod of discipline. Unconditional love trusts
where it cannot trace; and unconditional faith like
Job's accepts implicitly Divine Sovereignty. "Doubtless he is about to slay me, yet will I wait for (trust)
him" (Job 13 : 15; the Revised Version, "I have no
hope" runs counter to the whole current of the book.
A. B. Davidson on this says, "The word *to wait* hardly
has the sense of *to hope*, at least in this book." Cf.
6 : 11; 14 : 14; 29 : 21; 30 : 26, *Job* page 98).

"They also serve who only stand and wait" (Milton, On His Blindness). Since our Lord was "made perfect through suffering," we can neither serve nor succeed without suffering. Service to God is worth what it costs in submission to His blessed will whose Sovereignty touches everything in our lives. As "Lost time is never found again," lost opportunity to do God's will passes by forever. Real consecration keeps back no part of the price of entire submission to the King. His Kingdom depends in part for its realization on the subjects thereof subjecting themselves entirely to Him.

The Bible explicitly prescribes our journal of daily living the will of the Master. As love in its largest, deepest and truest is self-giving, then to what we give ourselves in love makes its fate ours. As consecration in heart, soul, and body identifies us with the destiny of God and the eternal future of His Kingdom, so by our sacrifice to it wholly we may settle for all eternity what and where our eternity shall be. Because the Bible is the Word of God, attitude to it makes it the Book of Human Destiny. God's future is absolutely insured in what He is and has given. His Word tells us how we may be assured that His future may be ours also. The most valuable insurance policy in existence is the promise of the Parousia that our Lord will come again and receive us unto Himself, that where He is we may be also.

VI. THE WORD OF GOD THE BREAD OF EVERLASTING LIFE

We become what we feed upon; and we last as long as it does. In all eternity we "shall live by every word proceeding out of the mouth of God." Food must be in keeping with the life it nourishes. The soul enjoying a blessed immortality forever feeds upon the Word of the ever-living Lord. Now man lives in a body. After the resurrection he will have a body living in and by the Spirit of Him who will raise it. Personal relations have growth and health by personal communications; and the Scriptures are the provision for this necessity of the Christian life.

Love should be our outstanding relation to God in response to His. His love for us being infinitely greater than ours for Him, His love must speak and ours should hear. In its chief aspect the Bible is the story of God's love for man. It is the Divine love-letter never growing old or stale. While that love passeth knowledge, it is always passing on knowledge to the beloved. While great in our creation, and still greater in our re-creation, we have in Christ the Bread of Greatness to feed upon. He said, "I am the bread of life." Let the bread of littleness be our steady diet, and we shrink to its proportions of insignificance. Feasting steadily upon the words "proceeding" (always present tense) "out of the mouth of God," and naturally and supernaturally the large-mindedness and the great-heartedness of Divine interests and achievements result, and are realized in personality.

God is so present in the Word of God that what seems past tense as it is written, becomes present tense as it is re-spoken to us. And the Scriptures being assimilable and digestible, they secure spiritual growth, health, and vitality. Though they deal with the most profound matters, through the help of the Accompanying Spirit who inspired them, they can be understood by the Re-born who reads them. There are exhaustless mines of wealth as well as vast expanses of truth in the Bible. Even in the most familiar passages new light and larger truths come forth again and again. It is not what we eat that feeds us; but what we digest. Alas, we may read the Word as we read newspapers, looking not for food and communion, but glimpsing it, galloping over its "Acres of Diamonds," and rushing past prepared banqueting halls where the Christ sits at the head of the table awaiting us. Surely it is worth while to give Holy Writ sufficient time and attention to receive its daily messages and build them into our being. The mind which is kept filled with the Word, preëmpted by the Truth of God, has a strength, a supernatural power that can come in no other way. Even the hardest commandments of God are the best of food. We get the nourishment in them by obeying them. Thus the Sovereign will of God steadies and stabilizes us, for we must first know the will of God to do it; and "he that doeth the will of God shall abide forever."

VII. THE BIBLE THE BOOK OF DIVINE FULFILMENT

God fulfils Himself in many ways. 1. His Nature fulfils itself in being true to Itself. 2. He fulfils Himself in all His relations. 3. His Sovereignty fulfils itself in the consummation of all His plans and purposes. 4. He fulfils Himself in all His activities. 5. His Eternal life is lived in the Spirit of everlasting

fulfilment. 6. He fulfils Himself in love and sacrifice.
7. And the eternal Tri-unity of the Godhead is Divine
Fulfilment.

1. The Word of God reveals that the Divine Nature
is adequate or sufficient in every way. His Nature fulfils itself in Holiness. This is the immaculate, flawless,
unapproachable majesty of ineffable purity in the god-
liness of God. Holiness is the first characteristic of
the Divine Nature. It stands first and last in the character of God. (See Isaiah 6: 3).

2. The first of all God's relations is within the Holy
Trinity. There the Father fulfils Himself eternally in
the Son and the Holy Spirit. And the Son fulfils
Himself in the Father and the Spirit, who also fulfils
Himself in the Father and the Son. All the Divine
relations in creation are the relations within the Trinity
carried into them. So He fulfils Himself in creation,
not by it. (See Matt. 5: 17; Acts 3: 18).

3. All fulfilment during the course of human existence reaches back to Divine Sovereignty. The Bible
unveils "The determinate counsel and foreknowledge
of God." His foreknowledge is simply His omniscience facing the future. So the Word shows that
"The purposes of God are ripening fast, Unfolding
every hour." (See Acts 2: 23; Rom. 8: 29; Eph.
1: 5, 11.)

4. All God's acts and activities perfectly correspond
with and express His nature and character, and are
thus His fulfilment in them. This might be called His
functional fulfilment. Each of the Persons of the
Trinity having a trinity of offices, God fulfils Himself
in all their outworkings. All Three Persons have a

share in every Divine act. For example, all Three took
part in Creation.   (See Gen. 1 : 1, 2; John 5 : 17; 1 :
3.) The most daring thing God ever did, was to create
personality, for its essential power of self-determination could cause it to throw away its fulfilment in God
by self-realization in sin, which is the prostitution of
the power of self-determination. Every created person
chooses either to make God the end of His existence,
or to put himself or something else in God's place, thus
plunging into the chaos of death, the lifeless life that
lives no more.

5. Life is not always the fulfilment of Personality:
sinful human life is anything but this fulfilment. But
the Divine is life eternal and always life fulfilling itself. The Scriptures set forth the sacrificial spirit as
eternal in the life of God. It was by eternal sacrificial
spirit that Christ offered Himself without blemish
unto God. (Heb. 9 : 14.) It was not merely by "the"
or "his" eternal spirit, for these words do not occur
in the original. The Persons of the Holy Trinity have
ever lived by eternal spirit manifest in sacrificial relation to each other. Thus they fulfilled themselves in
each other. From everlasting the Father and the Son
and the Holy Spirit have lived in that fellowship of
loving, personal sacrifices to each other. This life of
irrefrangible fellowship in the Godhead is ever because
of this sacrificial inter-fulfilment. The sacrificial fulfilment is eternal because it cannot be improved upon.

6. The Scriptures declare that "God is love." Then
He may fulfil himself in what He is. Sin did not
originate the need of sacrifice: love did, for without

sacrifice love would be fruitless sentiment instead of the self-giving of devotion which is the highest order of sacrifice. By disobedience to the sacrificial God and in breaking away from sacrificial relations of obedience to Him, man lost the means of his fulfilment. But the sacrificial fulfilment of God in Christ at Calvary makes available the Divine Bed Rock Strata as the foundation and substance of the substitute fulfilment, thus replacing the bottomless void of iniquity. By faith in the redeeming love of Christ human personality is included in and identified with the Divine fulfilment of love's perfect sacrifice.

"But now once at the consummation (fulfilment) of the ages hath he been manifested to put away sin by the sacrifice of himself. . . . He, when he had offered one sacrifice for sins for ever, sat down on the right hand of God; henceforth expecting till his enemies be made the footstool of his feet. For by one offering hath he perfected (consummated in character) for ever them that are sanctified" (Heb. 9:26; 10:12-14).

This is the fulfilment of Christ's infinite sacrifice in love for us and also the eternal outworking of His sacrificial spirit in us, thus completing the fulfilment of God's purposes both in our being and our becoming. This communication to and establishment of eternal life in us is that which enables partnership as co-workers with God and fellowship forever with Christ in that coming glory and triumph when "God is all in all."

7. The tri-unity of the Godhead is eternally a fulfilment of the Divine unity in infinite extent. All unity in creation comes from it. Redemption's fulfilment of

personal, human unity comes from that original unity in the Trinity, out of which issued the solution of the problem of sin's disunity in man. Iniquity is the one deadly foe to human unity and Divine fulfilment. Evidently our Lord saw this as He uttered His memorable "Passion Prayer" for unity:

"Neither for these only do I pray (make request), but for them also that believe on me through their word; that they may all be one; even as thou, Father, art in me, and I in thee, that they also may be in us, that the world may believe that thou didst send me" (John 17: 20, 21).

At Calvary that unity of the Trinity proved itself in the supreme test when upon the Son came the disruptive effect of sin. It did disrupt His physical life, and for the time it seemed to undo the Incarnation, putting Him out of this world into which He had come in love and grace to destroy the disruptive power of sin. When contradictory truths come to us, there is apt to be little unity in our thinking. A mediating truth should be sought. In fact the difficulty here lies in sin being not a truth but a lie, a lie as deep as hell. He who is the Truth suffered the asserted effect of the lie of sin that it was stronger than He. The mediating fact is, this could not happen except by Divine permission and the Saviour's submission. As Peter at Pentecost said: "Him, being delivered up by the determinate counsel and foreknowledge of God, ye by the hand of lawless men (men without the law) did crucify and slay" (Acts 2: 23).

It is well to notice the large amount of Scripture which this Spirit-filled preacher used in his sermon.

7

God's Word did not return unto him void. Would there not be more conversions from the preaching of today, if it contained and set forth more Scripture? There are at least ten times as many references to the fulfilment of God's Word as to any other fulfilment mentioned in the Scriptures. We do well therefore to let Inspiration explain the meaning, merit, and even the seeming contradictions in the death of Christ.

There must have been some great necessity for God's permission of sin to do as it did when it put Christ to death. Perhaps this necessity lies in providing or permitting the enablement of what Christ in Person became by His death. There was a deep necessity for the Word to become flesh that God might reveal His tri-Personality. There was also a deep necessity why Christ should suffer the effect of sin in His own Person and be raised from the dead to impart to man His sin-proof, sin-mastering, sin-uprooting, sin-exterminating life. This enabled Him to become *the New Covenant in Person with God,* as was promised, "I Jehovah . . . will form thee, and give thee for a covenant of the people, for a light of the Gentiles; to open the blind eyes, to bring out the prisoners from the dungeon, and them that sit in darkness out of the prison-house" (Isa. 42: 6, 7). Christ became this New Covenant for us when He sealed it with His own blood in far more than a ceremonial sense, for His blood, His life, seals us in giving to us His Eternal Life. Thus His suffering death created an entirely new situation. Before this God was the one sinned against: ever since He is the God who has borne our sins. Because of the unity of the Trinity, when Christ bore our sins, God bore them.

If we let the Scriptures speak, they will not "sacrifice" the unity of the Trinity, as some interpretations do. The final faith of some seems to be in *penalty*. The word does not once occur in the Scriptures. It would be more than passing strange that the main meaning, merit, and efficacy of what Christ underwent on the Cross consisted in penalty inflicted on Him by the Father, and this word expressing it be not found at all in the Bible! This faith in sheer penalty is the more astounding when we remember that penalty has never redeemed anyone. Satan has been suffering punishment for his sin for a long, long time, and he is just the same old devil still. And we are told that at last the hopelessly lost will suffer with the demons to all eternity without the least change for the better.

We may here note that most mistaken views of the meaning of Christ's death arise from proportionately mistaken views of the unity of the Trinity, or by leaving it out altogether. Let us examine some of the passages setting forth this matter.

On the way to Emmaus our Risen Lord explained to the two disciples the necessity for His death using the Greek verb *dei:* "Must (behooved it) not the Christ suffer these things and enter into his glory" (Lu. 24:26). What an exposition that was! "He interpreted to them in all the scriptures the things concerning himself." What think you did he say about Isaiah 53:10? "When his soul shall make a trespass-offering," or "Jehovah hath caused to meet (lit., made to light) on him the iniquity of us all." Much will depend on our interpreting content of mind how we explain the whole chapter. Christ had the full and true content of mind, for He had just fulfilled all that was written. Verse four is fulfilled by those who take it that God punished Christ for us: "yet we did esteem him stricken, smitten of God and afflicted." That was thought by many in the day He died; but also thought by penalists ever since. What a significant word it is!

It was sin and sinners who inflicted on the Saviour what He bore. "The wages of sin is death." Death is the punishment of sin, not of God. "Him who knew no sin he made to be sin on our behalf; that we might become the righteousness of God in him" (2 Cor. 5: 21). But Paul had just said "God was in Christ reconciling the world unto himself." Christ was made sin in effect; and only sin can produce the effect of sin. The Father did not and could not produce that effect, but He permitted it. And the Son also permitted that effect of sin upon His Person. His sacrificial blood being shed, it could also be transfused to blot out sin. All sin died in its effect upon Him. So to speak, the germs of sin find the surest death by the dead of its own kind. His blood became the antitoxin serum of Redemption. That was capitalized and made infinite in Christ for transmission to all who believe on Him.

Often does one hear the testimony: "Christ bore the full penalty of my sins on the Cross." The full penalty of sin is always *spiritual death;* and that punishment had already been borne by the one giving the testimony; and it was a penalty which Christ could not bear. Spiritually dying to the Father, the Holy Spirit, and to all the good Christ was seeking to do, would be the victory and fulfilment of sin. The unity of the Godhead would be forever broken up by the spiritual death of one of its constituent Members or Persons. Therefore the utmost sin could do, was to put to death His body; for instead of a spiritual death the Scriptures say that it was physical. "Being put to death in the flesh, but made alive in the spirit" (1 Peter 3:18).

Further, that absolute, transcendent unity of the Godhead we have been thinking about, certainly means nothing can happen to One Person of the Holy Trinity which does not thereby happen to some extent at least to the other Two Persons. Whatever the Father did to the Son, in similar measure He did to Himself. If He inflicted penalty on the Son, likewise He inflicted it on Himself. But when sin actually inflicted suffering on the Son of God, it was thereby inflicted on the entire Godhead. Otherwise its inter-personal, sacrificial unity was a shadow and no reality.

Instead of spiritually dying to the Father, the Word of God makes clear that He died unto or toward the Father: "Father, into thy hands I commend my spirit" (Lu. 23:46). As already said, each Person in the Triune Godhead shares in or responds to every act of each other. When the Father accepted Christ's sacrifice of Himself to the Father, the Son sent away or reciprocally dismissed to Him His spirit. The verb *"aphiēmi"* (Matt. 27:50) expresses just that. We may therefore conclude that the entire Trinity was true to Itself all through this strange experience; and that its sacrificial unity remained unshaken.

*   *   *   *

The Scriptures end as they began—with God on His throne. However, the final pages of Holy Writ present the Divine Sovereignty in an additional aspect —"The Throne of God and of the Lamb." Doubtless this is because the Divine Sacrifice of the Son had been consummated, and He had been received up into glory at the right hand of God. The Bible many times mentions the sacrifice of the Lamb of God, "Who being the effulgence of his glory and the impress of his substance, and upholding all things by the word of his power, when he had made purification of sins, sat down on the right hand of the Majesty on High" (Heb. 1:3).

It is the sacrifice of the Son which subdues all His enemies, and makes it possible for the Redeemed to overcome and to reign with Him. "And they overcame him (the Accuser) because of the blood of the Lamb, and because of the word of their testimony" (Rev. 12:11). The blind folly of would-be rulers and conquerors must always fail, for, according to the Word, only sacrificial personality is fit to reign, and finally will be allowed so to do. Only the sacrificial soul is destined to succeed with God in rule as in all else. At any rate the Bible is the Great Book of the triumph of Divine Sacrifice, and of the fulfilment of the unity on earth or in heaven which it makes Divinely possible.

Part Three

INSPIRATION IN PROCESS

Introduction: The main emphasis of Inspiration on its process.
The mystery of the meeting of the Divine and the human.

I. *Four ways in which God's Word comes to man:*
  1. Immediately in a voice that is heard.
  2. By Angels.
  3. By inspired spokesmen and writers.
  4. By the Son of God.

WE HAVE pointed out in the beginning that revelation differs from inspiration in that the main emphasis of revelation is on product, while the main emphasis of inspiration is on process. How the Holy Scriptures came into being is not at all easy to explain; for the Scriptures themselves do not and cannot tell us all of the mystery of the meeting of the Divine with the human in inspiration. But this is true in every instance where God in His transcendence and man in his finiteness come into contact. However, man is the instrument and the Holy Spirit is the Inspirer and Source of Holy Writ. This much at least is made plain to us.

I. Inspiration represents that there are four ways in which God speaks in His Word. 1. He speaks immediately to man, as to Adam in the Garden: "And they heard the voice of Jehovah God. . . . And Jehovah God called unto the man and said unto him . . ." (Gen. 3:8-10). It was in this way that the Decalogue was given: "And God spake all these words, saying, I am Jehovah thy God . . ." (Ex. 20:1-17).

At the baptism of our Lord God spake audibly (Matt. 3:17); and also at His transfiguration (Matt. 17: 5); and near the close of His ministry, "There came a voice out of heaven, saying, I have both glorified it (His name), and will glorify it again" (Jn. 12:28).

2. God also speaks by what the Old Testament calls "The Angel of Jehovah" (Gen. 16:7; 21:17; 22: 11). Also by "My Angel" (Ex. 23:23). And by "My Presence" (Ex. 33:14). And by "The Angel of his Presence" (Isa. 63:9). Finally by "The angel or Messenger of the Covenant" (Mal. 3:1).

3. God speaks by His prophets, the inspired spokesmen, and writers.

4. And He speaks by His Son. "God having of old time spoken unto the fathers in the prophets by divers portions and in divers manners, hath at the end of these days spoken unto us in a (his) Son" (Heb. 1:1, 2).

VII

PERSONAL PREPARATION FOR INSPIRATION

Introduction: The importance of the Divine foreplanning each personal life.

I. THE COMPETENCE OF GOD
The vast task of God in planning all. "Every life a plan of God."

II. THE WISDOM OF GOD'S CHOICES AND PREPARA-ATIONS
The necessity which God meets in this matter with infallible wisdom.

III. PREPARATION IN CREATION
Union with God the greatest human capacity.

IV. PREPARATION BY CLEANSING FROM SIN
Only purified personality able to unite with the Holy Spirit.

GOD has a most important task in fitting every person for his task in life. The Divine plans in this antedate all else in creation; for nothing can be well fitted for its place unless by being well planned for beforehand. Hence God must plan all or not at all. For this reason his foreplanning must leave out nothing which in any way affects our lives.

I. THE COMPETENCE OF GOD

Our God is competent in every way. He is as efficient in preplanning as He is in Providence, for His foreplanning is the prelude of His Providence. In all things and everywhere He is equal to His task. There is a famous sermon by Horace Bushnell on "Every life a plan of God" from the text, "I girded thee though thou hast not known me" (Isa. 45:5).

"That God has a definite life-plan for every human person, girding him, visibly or invisibly, for some exact thing, which it will be the true significance and glory of his life to have accomplished. . . . If there were any smallest star in the heavens that had no place to fill, that oversight would beget a disturbance which no Leverrier could compute; because it would be a real and eternal, and not merely casual or apparent disorder. One grain, more or less, of sand would disturb, or even fatally disorder the whole scheme of the heavenly motions. So nicely balanced, and so carefully hung, are the worlds, that even the grains of their dust are counted, and their places adjusted to a correspondent nicety. There is nothing included in the gross, or total sum, that could be dispensed with." [1]

God has had all the eternity of the past to plan what He will do in time. Though He has an infinity of it, He never wastes any time. Then, too, things cannot plan for themselves before they come into existence. All God's preplanning rests upon His absolute foreknowledge. "For whom he foreknew, he also foreordained" (Rom. 8:29). His foreknowledge would be untrue if all it meant were His intentions at that time. Since He foreknows all, He is able to predestinate all in wisdom. He plans what to do with and for every person. But His predestinations differ according to what He foreknows. Our safety lies in the grip of God on all things. Our salvation and well-being lies in this also. Very different is what He foreknows about different persons; and very different is His fore-

---

[1] *Sermons for the New Life*, pp. 10, 13. Charles Scribner's Sons.

knowledge of personal as compared with impersonal existences. He foreknows absolutely everything persons will be, will do, will respond to, and become; and He plans accordingly. God is a perfect Respecter of the integrity of personality, and will not plan before hand in an arbitrary way as though it were a mere thing and He a God of blind fate.

II. THE WISDOM OF GOD'S CHOICES AND PREPARATIONS

Necessarily God must choose beforehand all things for all persons which must be settled beforehand. He must choose our parents, the time and place of birth, talents and bent of personality. In His Divine Sovereignty He must foreordain and call every man to his task. "And whom he foreordained, them he also called" (Rom. 8:30). When men are to fill the place of inspired spokesmen or writers for Him, He must provide, arrange, and govern all the prenatal influences and forces which affect and mould them. Every person is born with a whole troop of predestinations at work upon him, but most of all God's.

In all God's choices there is infallible wisdom. He allows no man to drift into His service. He who drifts into some calling without the Divine appointment, does not belong there. What is not the Father's plan for our lives, cannot be the way of succss to us. Real personal fitness for and adptation to life's work always reaches back in its roots to the unerring purposes of Divine Sovereignty. God makes no square pegs for round holes.

III. THE PREPARATION IN CREATION

Before God inspires a man by His Holy Spirit, He must have made him capable of being inspired. When creating him there must be built into his being capacity for God. This capacity is that which makes an impassable gulf of differentiation between man and beast.

Of all human capacities which the Creator bestowed on man the greatest by far is capacity for God. And the greatest of all personal unions possible to man is with his God. But the greatest personal union in existence is in the Godhead between the inter-personalities of the Trinity, for that is a unity from all eternity and on infinite scale. Being made in the image and likeness of God has far deeper meaning than we are wont to realize. For one thing it involved being made or constituted with capacity for reciprocity with that triple unity of the Godhead. Man was therefore fashioned for unity within himself, for only a unity within personality can be in unity with another person, providing he too is a unity within. Clearly God created man for union with Himself and with fellow man. Here we come upon the foundational possibility, not only for the necessary union with the Holy Spirit in inspiration, but for all other unions within the wide scope of human life. A reflection of this capacity for union is seen in that the human mind may unite with another by telepathy, hynoptism, and in all the ordinary mental communions on various levels.

IV. PREPARATION BY CLEANSING FROM SIN

The beginning of human life, as inspiration tells us, was the beauty of a fine fellowship with the Maker.

Alas, that Divine-human union was short-lived. Iniquity thrust itself in, and the fine fellowship went out. Sin shattered the finest possibility which man possessed, for this Divine-human union was the foundation not only of man's religious life, but of all the highest and best possibilities for human progress, peace, and prosperity.

When iniquity had so deeply damaged this foundational God-ward possibility, the whole nature of human personality became corrupt, defiled, and unreliable. Only by the Divine cleansing from sin could man be restored unto union with God. Without this purging union with the Holy Spirit was quite impossible; for He cannot fill and inhabit any person controlled by iniquity. The Scriptures leave us in no doubt that *a man may have God's Spirit only as God's Spirit has him*. Hence only purified and purged personality can ever enter into inspirational union with God. All intimate service for the Divine is made possible through this cleansing from sin. This clears the way for union with the Holy Spirit and its resultant endowment of the individual for service. Inspiration for the writing of the Scriptures is not the only enduement by the Holy Spirit. There are as many and as varied Divine enduements as there are different tasks or callings. For each Divine service the Holy Spirit fits the worker through an appropriate endowment or gift, "Dividing to every man severally as he wills" (1 Cor. 12: 4-11). The outstanding character of the endowment of the Holy Spirit for the writing of the Scriptures we shall attempt to study a little later on in this discussion.

VIII

THE SOUL OF THE PROCESS OF INSPI-
RATION

Introduction: Union with the Holy Spirit as indispensable as
union with Christ.

I. THE MARVELOUS POSSIBILITIES OF THE DI-
VINE-HUMAN UNION
The light of the Incarnation on this union. Reason for
dwelling on the central Love of Christ in relation to all other
Divine-human unions.

II. REGENERATION ANOTHER IMPORTANT DIVINE-
HUMAN-UNION
Begotten from above a supernatural conception. All super-
natural matters stand or fall together.

III. THE SPECIAL FELLOWSHIP IN THE PROCESS OF
INSPIRATION
All such unions and fellowships reach back to those in the
Trinity.

As ALREADY said, the spirit of this process is the Holy
Spirit; but the soul of it is the union of God's Spirit
with the spirit of the person thereby inspired. In any
case a man can work the works of God only as he is
in union with Him. Union with and possession by the
Holy Spirit is indispensable to the process of the inspiration of the Book of books, even as union with
Christ is indispensable and foundational to the fruit-
bearing life for Him who said, "I am the vine and ye
are the branches . . . for apart from me ye can do
nothing" (Jn. 15:1, 5).

I. About *the vast importance and marvelous possibilities of this Divine-human union* the Scriptures have

much to say. They reveal that man owes his Redemption to it. This was the genius of the Incarnation by which the Redeemer was enabled to subject Himself to human conditions and necessities to the end of adapting and fitting Himself in Person to impart His sin-destroying spirit to sinners. His vicarious, sacrificial union with humanity put the Son of God under the whole load of human sin, that by the sacrifice of Himself He might "bear away the sin of the world." It was the infinite sacrifice of the Enhumanation which made possible Christ's going on to the infinite sacrifice of Calvary, for by this sin-death He dedicated Himself to the satisfaction of the Father in thus meeting the need to provide for sin's extermination and man's re-creation in the image and likeness of the sacrificial Son.

Why here dwell upon this? Because we never reach the soul of anything Divine in service to humanity until we uncover its fundamental relation to the greatest Divine service of all for us, the love of Christ passing all human knowledge in giving sinners eternal life at so great a cost. Then it is also important here to note that the process of inspiration in its very soul is in the image and likeness of the process of Divine Redemption by reason of its method of Divine-human union— the soul of both. There are four Divine-human unions: Creation of man, the Incarnation, Regeneration, and Inspiration. Here we consider union with Christ and Regeneration to be the same.

II. *Another important example of Divine-human union is the foundational reconstruction of man's na-*

ture involving, as it does, union with Christ. In this is a re-creation as supernatural in origin as the first creation of man, and involving vastly more in its Divine sacrifice. According to the Word of God regeneration is really a miraculous conception, which is the method of the Divine-human union in the Incarnation. Inspiration so expresses it in the original Greek: *"Gennaō anothen"* (Jn. 3:3), procreated, conceived, or begotten from above. *"Annagennaō"* (1 Peter 1: 23), "Having been begotten again, not of corruptible seed, but of incorruptible, by the word of God which liveth and abideth." This second word means re-procreated, re-conceived, re-begotten. The first word refers to being born of the Spirit, "Except one be born of water and the Spirit" (Jn. 3:5). And the second points to the birth from the seed of life eternal. Well may Christians earnestly contend for the supernatural conception of Jesus Christ, according to the Scriptures, for according to the same authority every Christian becomes such by being supernaturally conceived as Christ was. But He was not regenerated as we are, from sin. Every Christian being born again is "added unto the Lord" (Acts 5:14). Thus in personal nature every true Christian is a union of the human and the Divine. Well may we contend earnestly for the supernatural inspiration of the Scriptures, for they have come to us through the instrumentality of the Divine-human union like to that in our Lord's Incarnation and our own regeneration. This is the foundational fellowship-relation of Christianity.

III. Deliverance from the control of sin into the freedom of *fellowship-relation with God* enables the special Divine-human union necessary to the writing of the Scriptures. The production of them was not only a fellowship in truth, but for the universal fellowship in the Truth. May we repeat that every true fellowship must be rooted in that of the Holy Trintiy. Out of its resources came Redemption and the Inspired Word. This is why the soul of Christ yearned to unite all humanity in one family of God. The spirit and aim of Holy Writ is the same. Because the very soul of inspiration of the Word is the Divine-human union making it effectual, all devout regard for the Holy Scriptures helps to manifest this foundational fellowship with God. On the other hand anything which weakens faith in the Scriptures as the Word of God and in the inspiration which makes it so, means the crumbling of the fellowship-foundation under our feet, and betokens a spiritual condition and direction of movement which bodes ill for the answer of Christ's Great Passion Prayer for the unity of His followers in this Divine-human fellowship in His truth.

IX

THE PROCESS DEFINED AND EXPLAINEI

Introduction: The difficulty in defining the transcendent.

I. THE DEFINITION OF THE PRODUCT AND THI
PROCESS OF INSPIRATION
Scripture passages in which inspiration explains itself.

II. THE GOD-BREATHED SCRIPTURES
Passages concerning John the Baptist, Hosea, Joel, Jere
miah, and others.

III. THE SPIRIT CLOTHING HIMSELF IN MEN WH(
WROTE THE WORD OR SPOKE IT
Zechariah, Gideon, Amasai, and the New Testament parallel

THIS is a most difficult task. Wherever the Divin
and the human meet, unite, and work together, ther
is triple mystery. This is mainly because of the Divin
transcendence; for without its transcendence the Di
vine would not be Divine; and transcendence woul
not be such, if it were not unsearchable mystery
While we may not be able to explain all the myster
of its inspiration, thank God we have this Book o
books!

I. To define the process of inspiration necessaril
requires that first we define its product. Briefly this i
*the God-imparted nature and substance of the Scrip
tures.* They are foundationally, constitutionally, an
generically the product of an Inspirer and the inspired
for only truly inspired writers could produce truly in
spired writings. This means that the Primal Agent o
inspiration is the Holy Spirit. Those who define in

spiration as the Bible's power to inspire us, do not explain or even touch the real inspiration which produced the Word of God. With this we are concerned supremely.

While to some extent inspiration transcends human definition, and so far evades it, yet even a partial definition is of use to show the trend or direction of discussion. First, we may say, *The process of inspiration was that possession and actuation of the mind of man by the Holy Spirit whereby the message of Holy Writ was supernaturally received and faithfully imparted.* Second, we may say: *Inspiration in process was a Divine-human union and coöperation in which as usual the initiative was with the Divine: in this co-agency the Holy Spirit came upon chosen men, filled their minds to express the message of God found in the Bible.* Third, we may say: *In the process of inspiration God the Holy Spirit entered into union with chosen persons in such a way that their minds were exalted and enabled to receive and concur with the Divine Message to man, and in this coöperative confluence with the Divine Mind be carried onward in the coalescent activity of passing on the Divine Communication in words chosen by this union of God's Spirit with His elect agents.*

In the Bible the terms "Scripture," "prophecy," "law," and "oracles" are often used interchangeably and also frequently for the whole body of Holy Writ. Let us now look at a few passages of the Word of God in which inspiration to some extent defines or explains itself. "No prophecy of Scripture is of private (its own) interpretation. For no prophecy ever came (was brought) by the will of man: but men spake from God, being moved by the Holy Spirit" (2 Peter 1:21). Here the word translated "came" is the same as that translated "moved." This word in the original occurs also in the seventeenth and the eighteenth verses of the same chapter, and in the Revised Version is translated "borne" in each instance. This word used is *"phero,"* meaning to bear or carry along (active voice) or be carried or borne along (passive). The same word is used in Acts (second chapter, second verse) to describe the coming of the Pentecostal power with a sound like the "rushing" *(pheromenēs)* of a mighty wind. Concerning the inspiration of the prophets the form used by Peter is *"pheromenoi,"* which is in the passive voice, indicating that they were acted upon, were carried or borne along by a power not their own. This means not only that the prophecy came to them, but also that in the expression of it they were actuated or moved as by the Holy Spirit at Pentecost who came with a sound like as of the "rushing" of a mighty wind. It is here assumed that the same effect of the Holy Spirit would take place either in speaking or in writing a Divine message. It is of interest to note that Rotherham translates *"pheromenoi"* as "being borne along"; Moffatt, "being carried away"; Weymouth, "being impelled." Clearly this passage is an instance of what inspiration explains about its own process; and this should have more weight with us than uninspired explanations.

II. Another remarkable passage on the same subject says, "All" or "Every scripture is inspired of God" (R. V. marg.). Literally this means "God-breathed," *theopneustos* (2 Tim. 3:16). Here only does this rare word occur in the Bible. Evidently it means that God in inspiration was active in much the same way which He was in creating man, who was brought into being by what may be called either inspirational creation or creative inspiration. In both inspiration and creation the Communicating Person of the Holy Trinity, the Holy Spirit, was the Agent of impartation. By the inspired account we are informed that the Creator "breathed into his nostrils the breath of life (lives), and man became a living soul" (Gen. 2:7). Similarily God breathed into the minds of men the Word of Life, and the Scriptures became a living book, even as our Lord said about His words, "The words I have spoken unto you are spirit and are life" (Jn. 6:63). We have also the explanation, "The word of God is living and active" (Heb. 4:12). In the Greek the emphatic order is, "Living is the word of God and active." We read also that "By the word of Jehovah were the heavens made, and all the host of them by the breath of his mouth" (Ps. 33:6). Is this not another *theopneustos?*

Concerning John the Baptist we read, "The word of God came unto John" (Lu. 3:2). Here we have *epi* with the accusative, meaning the word came down from above and rested upon John. Filled with the Holy Spirit from his mother's womb, John needed not the Holy Spirit to come upon him, but rather the

Spirit's message in the Word of the Lord. A similar form of expression is used in Hosea 1:1; Joel 1:1; and Jeremiah 1:4. The Hebrew Word is *el* in all three cases: "The word of Jehovah that came unto Hosea"—"That came to Joel"—"The Word of Jehovah came unto me" (Jeremiah). The usual form in the Hebrew is that the Spirit of God or of Jehovah "came upon" the various prophets; and the verb generally used to express this is *"hayah,"* usually meaning to be, to exist. Perhaps this means the Holy Spirit comes to be, exists upon or in a man, and inspiration results.

III. We also read "And the Spirit of God came upon Zechariah" (2 Chron. 24:20). Here the verb used is *"lawbash"* or *"lawbesh,"* meaning to clothe. The marginal (R. V.) is "Hebrew, clothed itself with." Literally the meaning is, the Spirit of God clothed Himself (itself) with Zechariah. The same verb with the same sense is used in two other instances, Gideon, Judges 6:34, and Amasai, 1 Chronicles 12:18. For sheer beauty of description of the process of inspiration, where could this be equalled? Well, in the New Testament in at least one passage (Lu. 24:49). It was the Master Himself who said: "Tarry ye in the city, until ye be clothed with power from on high." Here the Greek verb used is *enduo,* to clothe. This is a good parallel to the Hebrew *lawbesh.* The Lord foresaw the tongues of flame, foreknew the sound of the Holy Spirit filling the room and clothing the disciples with this power from on high, and sending them out to the world-wide task of carrying the Word of God to all nations and peoples.

Part Four

INSPIRATION IN ADAPTATION

Introduction: There are three of these adaptations.

I. THE ADAPTATION OF THE HOLY SPIRIT TO IN-
DIVIDUAL WRITERS

II. THE ADAPTATION TO THE DIFFERENT KINDS
OF MATERIAL USED

III. ADAPTATION TO THE RELIGIOUS CONDITIONS,
CIRCUMSTANCES AND ATTAINMENT

CONTINUING our study of the process of inspiration,
we may note that it involves certain necessary adaptations of the Holy Spirit. Of course, any Divine-
human union is by adaptation and condescension. This
holds true in the work of the Holy Spirit in inspiration. There are at least three of these adaptations
which we may briefly consider.

I. First there is the adaptation of the Holy Spirit
to the individual writers with whom He entered into
coöperative union. There is differentiation we may
make, as we think of Moses, David, Isaiah, Jeremiah,
and Paul. No two of the thirty-five writers were precisely alike; and no two human minds are ever precisely the same in character and content. Necessarily God is limited by the interpreting content of
any mind He uses to speak for Him. So then the
first adaptation of the Divine in inspiration was to the
individual agents whom He employed.

117

II.   The second Divine adaptation was to the different kinds of material used in expressing the various messages of God.   Some was pure revelation; some was historical, some was prophecy, some poetry, some was compilation, some Gospel, and some Apocrypha.   Three different main types are found in the Old Testament and four in the New.   These will be enumerated later.

III.   The third adaptation to Divine inspiration was to the different religious conditions, circumstances, and stages of religious attainment, or the lack of it in persistent retrogressions.   As light may be adapted to the strength of the human eye or its condition at the time, so God was very gracious and patient in suiting His utterances to the varying degrees of spiritual vision.   In fact Divine inspiration always took into account the religious conditions and spiritual attainments to which God must address Himself from the days of Adam to the end of the first century.   Ever since those who turn to the Word of God find it adapted to human need and situation.

X

ADAPTATION TO INDIVIDUAL WRITERS

Introduction: Individuality enhanced in the service of God.

I. THE DIVINE AND THE HUMAN MUTUALLY EN-
ABLE AND LIMIT EACH OTHER
The Human enabled the Divine to use human language and
style; and the Holy Spirit was subject to the limitations of
human speech.

II. THE SOVEREIGN CHOICE OF INDIVIDUALS IN
MATCHLESS WISDOM
Dr. Warfield's explanation that adaptation is not corruption.
Instanced in Paul, Moses, David, and Isaiah.

III. ILLUSTRATION OF ADAPTATION IN THE INCAR-
NATION
The four adaptations in Creation, Inspiration, Incarnation,
and Regeneration give the setting of Inspiration.

GOD is the Great Respecter of human personality. This
is seen in various ways. He has never made two persons precisely the same—a variation we find in all His
creation. Personality, the highest type of life, has
each its own individuality in unrepeatability. The
more God uses a man, the more He enhances this
uniqueness of his individuality. For example, when
He saves and uses Paul, He accentuates his personality
in its originality of uniqueness. So it is with inspiration. Instead of lessening the marks of differentiation
in distinctiveness, rather it increases them. Adaptation
to inspiration is not obliteration of individuality.

As a human soul is the adaptation of the human
spirit to the condition of living in a body, there it pro-

duces its own distinctive features. There physical nature is enabled to live, move, and take on its own functions in keeping with the nature of its indwelling soul. Somewhat similarly the Holy Spirit integrates Himself in a human spirit by union with it, and by indwelling quickens it with His life. Thus it functions with and for Him in a distinct and original manner. Inspiration is a special instance of this general law of the Holy Spirit's relation to man.

I.   In inspiration this particular adaptation of the Divine and the human produced *mutual enablement and limitation*. As the soul enables the body, and is at the same time limited by it, so the Holy Spirit was both enabled and limited by the writers whom He inspires. This adaptation and limitation of the Holy Spirit in inspiration is at the same time an enablement of His human agent to speak or write the very thoughts of God in language as true to God Himself as it is to the individual writer. By means of this coöperative union with the writers of the Scriptures the Holy Spirit gave to each of them the Divine message intended for him to deliver. This enabled inspired spokesmen to say, "The mouth of the Lord hath spoken it" (Isa. 1:20; 40:5; 58:14; Jer. 9:12; Mic. 4:4). And the inspired writer, as he penned the sacred page in his own language and literary style, could affirm, "Thus saith the Lord" (Isa. 42:5; 2 Chron. 24:20).

All divine thought throughout the Holy Scriptures is unavoidably subject to the limitations of human language, while at the same time God is thus enabled to utter Himself in word of our word, speech of our speech, expression of our expression. This enablement was all the more potent because the Divine union with the human soul was by means of inhabitation. The Holy Spirit is God the Inhabitant. The adaptation being thus personal and internal, the enablement of God made it possible for Him to coöperate even in the choice of the words used in conveying His message.

II. *The matchless wisdom with which the Father in sovereign choice selected and prepared* those for the writing of the Scriptures is manifest. We can see how well they were adapted to their tasks and times. The invisible cog-wheels of Divine Providence turning in the intricate machinery of omniscient wisdom have visible results in most wondrous adaptation of persons and communications. Dr. Warfield has a fine word about providential preparation in men as well as in matter. He well says:

"If God wished to give His people a series of letters like Paul's, He prepared a Paul to write them; and the Paul He brought to the task was a Paul who spontaneously would write just such letters.

"If we bear this in mind, we shall know what estimate to place upon the common representation to the effect that the human characteristics of the writers must, and in point of fact do, condition and qualify the writings produced by them, the implication being that, therefore, we cannot get from man a pure word of God. As the light that passes through the colored glass of a cathedral window, we are told, is light from heaven, but is stained by the tints of the glass through which it passes; so any word of God which is passed through the mind and soul of a man must come out discolored by the personality through which it is given, and just to that degree ceases to be the pure Word of God. But what if this personality has itself been formed by God into precisely the personality it is, for the express purpose of communicating to the word given through it just the coloring it gives? What if the colors of the stained-glass window have been designed by the architect for the express purpose of giving to the light that floods the cathedral precisely the tone and quality which it receives from them? What if the Word of God that comes to His people is framed by God into the Word of God it is, precisely by means of the qualities of the men formed by Him for the purpose through which it is given? . . . We must remember that He is the God of providence and of grace as well as of revelation and inspiration, and that He holds all the lines of preparation as fully under His direction as He does the specific operation which we call technically, in the narrow sense, by the name of "inspiration." The production of the Scriptures is, in point of fact, a long process, in the course of which numerous and very varied Divine activities are involved, providential, gracious, miraculous, all of which must be taken into account in any attempt to explain the relation of God to the production of Scripture. When they are all taken into account, we can no longer wonder that the resultant Scriptures are constantly spoken of as the pure Word of God." [1]

Dr. Warfield has thus well set forth the truth that adaptation which really enables the message to be understood, is *not a corruption of it*. Looking back we see that when the revelation of Law was needed God's providence had ready the legal talent of Moses, gifted

[1] *Revelation and Inspiration,* p. 101.   Oxford University Press.

adequately in natural endowment, and trained in both the schools and the royal court of Egypt. Inspired of God he became the greatest law-giver of all time. We behold David also who was similarly trained for his task in the school of trouble, educated in "the university of adversity." His poetic soul passed on the inspired message found in the Book of Psalms, which has been a devotional textbook to godly-minded men ever since. Isaiah was similarly poetic and prophetic. Josephus tells us he was of royal lineage. With lips cleansed and soul inspired he became the great prophet of the Messiah, prophesying of the coming King of kings and Lord of lords with a precision as if he were recording history. For the New Testament certain messenger-men of the Messenger from heaven did write the most important history and biography in all the world. Flawlessly did they portray His Person, and faithfully reported they the words of Him who spake as never man spake. We may fitly note that not a Biblical writer was without natural endowment and supernatural enduement. Never did God trust to human talents alone; and never was an empty head inspired or used to utter or write the Word of God.

There was, then, mutual adaptation enabling coördination of the Divine and each human helper. The efficiency of the union of the Mind of the Spirit with the human mind is manifest in the product of inspiration. Evidently all the Scriptures came through this competent adaptation of the natural and the supernatural.

III. It may help us to recognize a *similar adaptation of the Infinite to the finite in the Incarnation.* Not Mary apart by herself in parthenogenesis, nor the Infinite Holy Spirit apart by Himself; but the Virgin and vital union of the two brought forth the Marvel of all marvels, "the Only Begotten God," or "God Only Begotten," *"monogenes theos"* (John 1:18). From that central moment in the history of eternity when the Word had become flesh, our Lord's humanity was thenceforth in subservient union with His Deity. So also in the history of the process of the inspiration of Holy Writ there was from first to last complete subservience or concurrence of the human with the Divine in thought and thinking, in utterance and expression.

The union of the supernatural with the natural in inspiration finds still further illustration in the Incarnation. For example, it was not the Person of the Son of God which came into existence by the miraculous conception, for the preëxistent Son was God the Word without beginning. In a similar way Divine Truth was not brought into existence by inspiration, for this Truth had always existed, but became at the time of the action of the Holy Spirit the thought and expression of those inspired. As there was the preëxistent Son before His Incarnation, so was there the preëxistent Truth of God before inspiration. Inspiration was the transmission, not the origination of this Truth, even as the Incarnation originated, not the Person of the Son of God, but His enhumanation. After the Word became flesh, He was not less God the Son.

After Divine Truth became the Holy Scriptures, it was not less the Word of God.

In the four great Divine-human unions the marvel of Divine adaptation is well worthy of note. How sufficiently and perfectly God adapted Himself to man made in His image and likeness, and then how savingly He adapted Himself to man the sinner. From the beginning how fully did the Divine Son adapt Himself to human life, nature, and needs! The re-begetting or re-creation of the lost is Grace's adaptation in reconstruction to the greatest need of man which Grace ever filled because foundational. When we look upon the Divine adaptation in inspiration in company with the other three adaptations, we see inspiration's native setting. Certainly God stooped a long way to the level of man's mental and spiritual powers to make him the mouthpiece of His Message to all who might feed on His Word. That was a wondrous condescension by which the Holy Spirit entered into personal union with chosen men; for this created its own possibility, and, as we have seen, was the soul of the process of inspiration.

XI

ADAPTATION TO MATTER AND MODE OF MESSAGE

Introduction: Inspiration subjected the material to the specific Divine design.

I. THE INDISPENSABLE NEED OF DIVINE LAW

God alone could give the Law which regulated and prohibited. The reason for more prohibitions than directions. The two fundamental purposes in the Law. Grounded in unchanging Divine faithfulness.

II. THE LEVITICAL CODE PROVIDED A WORKING BASIS WITH GOD FOR SINNERS

It instituted a high order of religion. The inability of the worshipper supplemented.

III. THE BOOK OF THE PROPHETS

Their messages directly from God. True and false prophecy.

IV. THE HAGIOGRAPHA

Much of this compilation mirroring religious experience. Inspired thought of the communion of the saints. Three types intermingle.

V. THE GOSPELS IN NEW TESTAMENT INSPIRATION

The Redemptive revelation of God manifest in the flesh. Parallel Four of them because important without parallel.

VI. THE GENESIS AND EARLY GROWTH OF THE CHURCH

The Ministry of the Spirit manifest. The inspired church.

VII. THE EPISTLES

The letters not less profound than other Scriptures. They set forth spiritual insight into the Christian life and appraisal of Christ.

126

VIII. THE APOCALYPSE
This a fulfilment of promise of Inspiration "to show things
to come." The Parousia and Eschatology in general.

As ALREADY noticed, there are seven distinct types of
material and order of message in the sixty-six books
of the Bible. They are not, however, so distinct that
they do not run into each other. For example, the so-
called Books of the Law are also prophecy and history.
The five books of Moses called the Pentateuch are
the beginning of successive steps of the Self-revelation
of God. That these five Books of the Law were pre-
served in written form, is mentioned near the close of
the last one.

"And it came to pass, when Moses had made an end
of writing the words of this law in a book, until they were
finished, that Moses commanded the Levites, that bare
the ark of the covenant of Jehovah, saying, Take this book
of the Law, and put it by the side of the ark of the covenant of Jehovah your God, that it may be there for a witness against thee" (Deut. 31 : 24-26).

Throughout the whole course of the Scriptures their
Divine inspiration subjected not only the Pentateuch
but all the rest of the material of the Scriptures to the
specific design of God's purposes in and along with
them. For this reason the subject matter varies from
book to book according to the Divine adaptation of
message to the needs *as God saw them*. This gave the
Law the primary or introductory place after the story
of creation and the swift disaster of sin. But for
iniquity human nature could have been intuitively a
law unto itself in relation to God and all else. Sin and

9

the law condemning it stand therefore in this initial setting in the age-long course of the matters in subsequent Biblical statements.

I. The condition and the character of human lives during this early period manifest *the indispensable need of Divine Law.* Only God knew what it should be and was in a position to give it. Men were acting and judging according to wilful want, deranged desires, and discordant impulses all running contrary to man's need and relation to God. The Law itself was prescribed regulation of life in God and the prohibition of evil affecting it. In the Law fundamental necessities of this life were coupled with the elimination of malignant evils. Coming after sin had infested and overspread all human life, the Decalogue or the "Ten Words" from God consisted largely of what He forbade. Being addressed to sinners the "shalt-nots" outnumbered the "thou-shalts."

Two fundamental requirements are found in the Ten Commandments—faithfulness to life in God, and the regularity of its functioning or working. This regulative religious and moral law prescribed a reciprocity of righteousness with the righteous God; and it also required undeviating perpetuity in following out the correspondence of a righteous life. The law centered in right relation to God, and sought to bring all other relations in conformity with the Divine Will. Sin did not interrupt the regularity of natural law, for sin is personal and natural law reigns over the impersonal. Only in the personal realm could iniquity overthrow the reign of law, because it could change personal nature only. Sin is a contradiction to law, a personal growth in unfitness for, antipathy to, and unfaith in God. In the New Testament this opposition to God's law is called *"anomos"* and *"anomia,"* meaning lawlessness and its anarchy. Paul, Peter, and John so describe iniquity's attitude to God and His law. (1 Tim. 1 : 9; 2 Peter 2 : 8). John uses *"anomia"* in the sense of violation of law and wickedness.

Divine Law is grounded in the faithful, unchanging way God's nature works in being true to Himself and in all His relations. To man's blinded mind and deranged condition God comes with the revelation which His law makes as to His purpose in man and the appointed channel of life in him. "This do and thou shalt live." While there is no grace in the law itself, there was grace in the giving of it, that man might thereby know not only his actual state and condition through sin, but also convicted by it he might turn to God for remedy of the great evil into which he had fallen. The Law therefore was the Divine revelation of man to himself, what he should be in nature, spirit, and activity, his helplessness and need of grace.

II. While Sinai's legal code was moral and religious, *the Levitical was added to provide a basis of working relation between sinners and God.* This recognized the guilt of sin, and provided a way by which man might come unto God for forgiveness and worship. On the one hand there was man's inability to restore himself, and on the other a holy God with whom he must have relation either in judgment or in restoration.

The Levitical directions were wonderfully complete, not only in instituting its basis, but also in directing the practice of a high order of religion. This may be seen in the fundamental conception of the supernatural, personal God, holy and just yet abounding in grace. Moreover this Law recognized that a sinner had neither the right nor the ability to come to the God of transcendent holiness. A great feature growing out of the personal nature of the Most High was the Divine covenant. In this He agreed that He would fill his place as their God, while they made this possible by reciprocation in obeying His statutes, and offering appointed sacrifices. The practice of this constituted Israel a theocracy, a priestly kingdom, a holy nation.

In these ceremonial observances God in condescension supplemented the inability of the worshipper. When the offering of Divinely appointed sacrifice was made for sin, God took the offering and covered the sin with this covering or atonement. It was not by chance that the sin-offerings were made in blood, for God had made this the most sacrificial thing in created life in this world. The sacrificial ministry of the blood in the body fitted it preëminently for an offering to God. Not only did this foreshadow the Divine sacrifice in the Son, but it was intended to institute and keep before the covenant people the sacrificial order of living which should characterize their conduct. One may well note the high appreciation of the Law in the Old Testament, for example, in the One Hundred and

Nineteenth Psalm. Thus one inspiration devoutly praised another.

III. *The Book of the Prophets* was the second in the order of inspiration's adaptations in Scriptural material. These prophets were man not only in touch with human life: they had also been dwelling with God. Filled with and endowed by the Spirit of God they received their messages directly from Him. Thus they were fitted to be His forth-tellers, uttering his word faithfully at any cost, though usually what was spoken by them found its way into written form. Foretelling or predicting, though vitally important betimes in identifying the prophet as speaking for God, occupied in extent a minor place.

In any matter what the true prophet said was never the mere product of his own mind. While their messages were outpourings of the heart, prophecy itself declared that when any one prophesied out of his own heart, or when prophets spake a vision of their own hearts (Ezek. 13:1-3), or followed their own spirits (Jer. 23:16), they were false prophets. While there were schools of the prophets, in them they were trained but not made by them, even as a theological seminary of today cannot manufacture ministers of the Gospel. We have neither time nor space here to discuss the different types of prophecy, nor how the messages came by vision, trance, dream, or by angels.

IV. *The Hagiographic is the Third Body of Old Testament Writings.* In this order there was some revealed truth; but mostly matter of a devotional character written by men in communion with God, and mirroring what God had made known in religious experience. Sometimes it was mainly if not altogether compilation. These holy writings were the result of the Holy Spirit's inspiration of the communion of the saints in outreach of heart, mind, and soul after God. In a word, the Hagiographa were the inspired thoughts concerning God's general but also immediate contact with human life, and the religious reaction with its main emphasis on Godward experience. Thus God was seen, not only in His providential care, but also in His gracious helpfulness in dealing with the sin which had tangled up the very warp and woof of life.

Between these three main orders of revelation-material there is no hard and fast division, for they more or less intermingle. While the Psalms are Hagiographa, they praise the Law and contain Messianic prophecies. The Book of the Law had much prophetic material, and Moses was classed equally as Law-giver and Prophet. Isaiah was prophetic, didactic, and poetic. While Jeremiah is mainly prophetic, in Lamentations he is Hagiographic in expressing godly experience.

V. *The Gospels introduce us to New Testament Inspiration.* All the New Covenant literature in varying way and measure is nevertheless in the main the Memorabilia of Jesus Christ. In it is fulfilled the promise that the Holy Spirit would bring all things to the remembrance of the apostles and disciples in their ministry. Of first importance in this was what Jesus revealed, said, and did. The Gospels are more than four inspired pictures of the Person and Life of our Lord, for they are the Redemptive Revelation of God manifest in the flesh, dying, rising, ascending, and coming again. Here the adaptation of inspiration reaches the highest order in situation and material. The Gospels could be written only by men with the rich background of the Christian life and with the Gospel interpreting content of mind along with the Holy Spirit's superhuman help. There are four parallel Gospels because of their unparalleled importance in material. Each was addressed and adapted to a particular group though not exclusively so. The Synoptics contain the story as it had been preached hundreds of times in each others' hearing. Writing later John supplements those things which establish the Deity of the Man of Nazareth. (Jn. 20:31.)

VI. *The Genesis and Early Growth of the Church* is so well told by the physician Luke, it has been called "The Acts of the Holy Spirit." With this it might also be called the Gospel in Action. Because of Christ's Death and Resurrection the Spirit was enabled to enter upon a new era of Christ-impartation. Pentecost ushered in that marvelous manifestation of power from on high, enduing the disciples to carry on Christ's conquest in all the world for the Redemption of mankind. It is the story of the inspired church.

VII. In *the Epistles we have another adaptation in the material of Scripture writings.* Letters are usually not expected to be very deep. Not so with these!

Paul's Epistle to the Romans has been named the profoundest writing in existence. The Epistle to the Hebrews by an unknown author is the nearest to formal theological statement to be found in all the Bible. While some of these letters are mostly concerned with pastoral interests, they never fail to reveal deep theological insight and the after-thought in direct sequel to the Gospel account and always in devoutest appraisal of Christ and the Christian life.

VIII. *The Apocalypse* is supplementary to John's Gospel and Letters and to the whole Bible, for that matter, for it is the final or concluding fulfilment of the promise of the Lord that the Holy Spirit would "show them (disciples) things to come." While the Parousia is mentioned very many times all through the New Testament, the Apocalypse by Divine inspiration pictures succeeding ages with varying vicissitudes of victory and defeat, of faithfulness and of recession to the last great "falling away," "the Second Coming" and the Final Judgment. This unveiling of the stages and the culmination of the whole course of Christian history makes it a most fitting eschatology or account of things to come. It is the only Scripture which in the twentieth chapter mentions the Millennium by name, and seems to give it wholly over to the reign of the martyrs. The manifest apostasy of today has turned large numbers of Postmillennialists into Amillennialists. So with such the choice now is: Premillennialism or no Millennium at all. The Book ends thus: "He who testifieth these things saith, Yea: I come quickly. Amen: Come Lord Jesus."

XII

ADAPTATION TO RELIGIOUS CONDITIONS

Introduction: Varied conditions, fluctuation of receptivity, change of spiritual level, decline or advance of religious interest call for adaptations.

I. ADAPTATION TO PROGRESS
Not progress toward the truth, but in it. The Bible inspired from start to finish. It is the true message of God adding truth to truth. Adoption of error not adaptation of truth.

II. PAUL'S ADAPTING HIMSELF BUT IN LOYALTY TO THE TRUTH
Held back no essential truth.

III. STATUTES GIVEN THAT WERE NOT GOOD
Ezekiel's explanation. Directions about polygamy given by Moses.

IV. GOD'S PATIENT ADAPTATIONS IN LEGISLATION FOR THE UNSPIRITUAL
Allowance made according to light.

V. THE CONTRAST IN PRAYERS RECORDED
Stephen's compared with Zechariah's. The situation of the latter. The adaptations to the needs as God saw them.

THE THIRD ADAPTATION of the Holy Spirit in the inspiration of the Scriptures was to the varying religious conditions, capacities, and changing needs and circumstances of those to whom the Divine messages came during some fifteen hundred years. The spiritual levels varied from time to time. In the different periods the religious situations altered very much. Often there was decline instead of advance. In view of these differing situations there were divine adaptations in the communications from God. Spiritual receptivity

135

fluctuated throughout all these years. As the limitations of the taught are at the same time the limitations of the teacher, so the limitations of those to whom the Word of God came, were at the same time the limitations of Divine inspiration.

I. Then, too, *there was of necessity progress in the Scriptures.* Their whole message could not be given at once. Progress is made by adding truth to truth; but it cannot be in truth and at the same time progress toward or in the direction of the truth. The reliability of the Bible lies in its being the inspired Word of God from the start. The first line of Holy Writ is as true as the last. "In the beginning God created the heavens and the earth," cannot be improved upon as a statement of fact. That Christ is coming again, is as true as He is the truth (Gen. 1:1; Rev. 22:20). Inspiration would not really be of God and by the Spirit of Truth, if its message to man proceeded with admixture of truth and of untruth.

Adoption of error cannot really be regarded as adaptation of truth. Adapting truth to the actual conditions found is not adopting the evil, immorality, or unrighteousness which the conditions show. The faithful prophets did not dissemble, condone ungodliness, nor propagate untruth. While Divine light was adapted to the state and strength of spiritual vision, never in Scripture was this light further darkened by presenting falsehood as truth or sin as other than hateful in the sight of God.

II.   That was *a Divine adaptation in spirit when Paul was all things to all men,* that he might win some to Christ, to salvation, and to truth; yet no man ever preached the pure Gospel in greater faithfulness.   His loyalty to truth was unsurpassable and invincible. When he told the Athenians that "the times of ignorance God overlooked; but now commandeth men that they should all everywhere repent" (Acts 17:30), he did not hold back from them the essential truth of Christ's resurrection, because his hearers were anything but disposed to accept it.

III.   Ezekiel tells us that when the wayward Jews rejected God's laws, profaned His Sabbaths, and practiced idolatrous rites, *He could not direct them as though they were faithful to Him.*   For this reason Jehovah says: "Moreover I gave them statutes that were not good, and ordinances whereby they should not live" (Ezek. 20:25).   Reading the whole section (verses 18-28) we see that this was the limit in adaptation to deplorable conditions due to adoption of unspeakable evils and even pagan crimes.   When similar unfaithfulness existed in Moses' day, he gave directions about divorce, polygamy, and limited retaliation. This shows how far beneath the level of the Decalogue they had descended in evils which God directed to be restrained, when He would prefer to abolish them altogether.

The adaptation of the Old Testament as a whole was to starlight and coming dawn before the Light of the World appeared in Jesus Christ.   When the Master was inquired of why Moses provided for divorce, He explained: "Moses for the hardness of your heart suffered you to put away your wives; but from the beginning it hath not been so" (Matt. 19:8). The argument used for monogamy went back to creation. "God made a male and a female," not one man and two or more women. Merely that in the beginning male and female were created could as well prove polygamy as monogamy.

IV. When sin had tangled up all the relations and affairs of life, *God patiently adapted legislations for the unspiritual people* so sorely lacking in moral discrimination and appreciation even of God Himself. Jesus taught that God had ever made allowance according to light, and that judgment was "more tolerable" for those in relatively dark ages before the Light of Life and the Law of Love became manifest in Him.

To enter here into the various situations and the corresponding needs of allowance in Old Testament stages and levels of religious conditions is not possible. The so-called imprecatory psalms were not so much blind bitterness as vigorous, righteous indignation against the enemies of God. "No virtue is safe that is not enthusiastic"; and anger against unrighteousness and those guilty of it was Old Testament enthusiasm for Jehovah. As the family and not the individual was the unit of social and religious life, till late in the Old Testament period, children were often included in maledictions and judgment. In the New Testament

Paul in speaking of the harm which Alexander the Coppersmith did, righteously judged that "The Lord will render to him according to his works" (2 Tim. 4: 14). So was it said of Judas that he "went to his own place." Each case is but the inevitable end truly recorded.

V. Some have unfairly contrasted *the dying prayers of Stephen and our Lord with that of Zechariah* who said: "Jehovah look upon it and require it" (2 Chron. 24: 22). It was not bitter unforgiveness which so moved the prophet; rather it was desire for the vindication of the integrity of his message as from the Lord and the reality that God had spoken by him. When the Spirit of the Lord "clothed Himself with Zechariah," he then brought the message from Jehovah rebuking the people because they had forsaken Him, and their doing this evil made it impossible for Him to prosper them while serving "Asherim and the idols." Then came the Divine pronouncement of judgment by Zechariah. Whereupon the people at the command of the king were stoning the prophet to death. It was not a question of forgiveness, but whether or not Zechariah was a fraud, a false messenger of God. At that moment this was the situation. Now the father of the prophet, Jehoiada, a great and good man, a priest of God, had greatly befriended King Joash. When the priest died, King and people brought the wrath of Jehovah upon Judah for the guilt of turning utterly away from the Lord and into paganism. God sent prophet after prophet to bring them back, but all in vain. Then Zechariah the son of

Jehoiada the priest was specially anointed or clothed in the Spirit of God, and was sent with the divine rebuke and announcement of judgment. The only response of King Joash was to command the death of Zechariah as a false prophet. So the people stoned him to death in the very court of the temple, while he prayed with his last breath that God would vindicate Himself, His judgment, and His prophet. And the answer came in swift vengeance upon those guilty of slaughtering the prophet. It came in such a way that showed Jehovah looked upon the murder of His messenger as added and vexatious outrage, and that Zechariah was His true spokesman of His righteous judgment upon the king false to Him and upon the ungodly people as well.

Enough has here been written to show that the adaptation of inspiration does not mean that God can be flouted to His very face ignominiously, and that nothing would be done by Him about it, for He is not shown to be a pusillanimous Deity. Where mercy becomes worse than useless and patience ceases to be a virtue, God knows it and acts accordingly. There is also the inspired adaptation to the need of judgment and to definite fulfilment of His Word pronouncing this. The various adaptations of God's Word were to the varying conditions and needs *as He saw them*. In the New Testament period the adaptation was to the fulness of time and the need of the Personal Word to be sacrificed for the world's Redemption. The New Testament Message centers in this Divine Denouement.

INSPIRATION IN PSYCHOLOGY

Introduction: Some think no religious matter well treated till psychology is heard from.

I. DEFECTS OF PSYCHOLOGICAL TREATMENT
Single powers taken for the whole of personal activity as Consciousness, Reason, and Will. The old water-tight-compartment psychology dies hard.

II. IT IS THE PERSON WHO IS INSPIRED AND NOT MERELY THE MIND
Inspiration does not in reality consist in the consciousness of it. Consciousness runs along the line of personal activity. Place of Attention.

III. INSPIRATION MADE MEN MESSAGE-CONSCIOUS
Inspired men wholly intent on transmitting God's message. Automatic consciousness. Psychology not able to solve the mystery of Divine inspiration.

IV. THE FOUNDATIONAL INSUFFICIENCY HERE IS ITS NATURALISTIC LIMITATION
No one writing Scripture today by Divine inspiration. Cannot therefore observe that experience. Inspiration quickened and exalted human powers.

V. HELP OF THE EXPERIENCE OF BEING SPOKEN TO BY GOD
But to be spoken to is not to be inspired.

IN CLOSING this discussion of the subject of Divine inspiration, it may be well to look briefly at the psychology of it. For some time it has been the fashion to consider no religious matter well treated till psychology and the religious consciousness are heard from. This requirement has its difficulties; for there

141

are many subjects of theology not within the realm of human experience and observable processes thereof.

I. There are also *difficulties due to defects of current psychological treatment.* For example, some still insist on psychology as bounded by consciousness, as though consciousness includes every process of the human mind; just as other persons include all personal action in that of the will. Moreover psychology in the larger sense is concerned with all the powers and processes of the psyche, the soul, the person.

The old water-tight-compartment psychology dies hard. God speed its demise! It may help to insist once more that personal powers do not initiate action, for that is personifying them. It is the person who is conscious, not consciousness itself. Consciousness is really an abstraction; and abstractions are as dead as Julius Cæsar. The will does not govern persons, and it is the person who wills and not the will itself. The ear does not hear, and the eye does not see: we ourselves do these things by using these faculties or powers. Consciousness is personal awareness.

II. This leads us to note that it is not the human mind which is really inspired: it is in fact *the person who thinks, is inspired, and enters into union with the Holy Spirit,* though we often speak loosely of the Mind of the Spirit uniting with the human mind. In any case and as a matter of fact inspiration does not consist in the consciousness of it; and therefore it cannot be measured by human consciousness.

Usually personal consciousness is directed along the line of the activity in which the person happens to be engaged. Normally, an inspired person is conscious of what he is saying or writing, just as an uninspired man is conscious of what he is doing. One may be reading a book and getting nothing out of it. He may remember not a word or an idea in it, because his consciousness and attention have strayed away to other things. The latter are the things he is really doing or thinking about. In any case, the more thoroughly one is absorbed in anything, and the more he is in union with God, the less struggle is there to do the Divine will and keep his mind upon the doing of it. Then, of course, the more will the human consciousness be upon what it is the will of God for him to do. However, both God and attention control this consciousness.

III. Because the writers of Scripture were subservient to the Holy Spirit, they were not self-conscious, but rather *God-conscious or message-conscious*. Perhaps for the time being they were not even conscious that they were inspired, for the more important the work being done, the more consciousness is normally fastened upon it. Both attention and awareness then tend to be riveted upon the important work in process. Perhaps in inspirational concurrence and in confluence of activity with the Holy Spirit the writers of Scripture were wholly intent upon uttering or expressing the message according to the dominating though coöperating urge along with the Holy Spirit in them and they in Him. On the other hand, no man works at his best in highest efficiency even in inspiration unless do-

10

ing much of it *automatically*. There is an automatic attention and consciousness or awareness which together work for more satisfactory efficiency. It may be that in inspired activity the power of consciousness is automatically used so as to be entirely taken up with what is said or written, even as it would be in uninspired writing or speaking. Doubtless an exclusive absorption of consciousness is possible in either inspiration or in uninspired activity. There is therefore nothing in personal consciousness to account for the nature, process and value of the coöperation of the Divine-human mystery of inspiration which produced the Word of God to man. We may delve into that mountain of mystery with all our might; but in the end we come out by the same hole we went in.

IV. The insufficiency of psychology in explaining the mystery of inspiration is its naturalistic limitations. Doubtless we shall have to wait for the next world to have a psychology of the supernatural. In attempting to discuss inspiration the best we can do is to project natural principles into the supernatural. We are today unable to study the process of the experience of persons who are writing inspired Scriptures, for none are to be found. We are told that "The spirits of the prophets are subject to the prophets" (1 Cor. 14:32). Perhaps this means that while they were submissive to the Holy Spirit, they were not compelled. We know that inspiration was not like hypnotism in which memory and consciousness were suppressed. Instead of suppression the Divine Spirit quickens, exalts, and ennobles human powers.

V. Perhaps the nearest our psychology can come to inspiration is to compare *the experience of being spoken to by God*. The best verification and identification of this is the proof in Divine relief and uplift. A man came for the first time to the grave of his mother who had led him to Christ, sacrificed to the utmost for his education, inspired him to enter on preparation for the ministry, and in no way had failed to be the utmost in ideal Christian motherhood. In utter desolation of soul he threw himself upon that sacred mound. He was immediately spoken to: "Why seek the living among the dead?" Immediately he sprang up to look around for the speaker. No one was in sight in that lonely spot. Then it began to dawn upon him that it was no external voice which had spoken, but an inner, different, quiet voice which had called to him. That it was no trick of his subconsciousness suggesting these words did not occur to him, he was so certain that another had asked this question. All at once the meaning of it came home to him. Immediately a great joy filled his soul. He ceased thinking of his mother as under the clods. How could she be there? She had gone home. God must have said it, it was so Divinely timely, appropriate and helpful. Of course, he was not inspired: he was but spoken to; but it was the experience of God's short-cut way of talking into the ears of the soul. Now he knows more about how God can use internal, immediate impact without the help of external media. Now he knows that God still speaks to men; and he finds it easy to believe that He spake into the souls of those whom He inspired to be the writers of the Sacred Oracles.

LITERATURE

GENERAL REFERENCE

Hasting's Dictionary of the Bible, "Prophecy," by A. B. David-
son, Vol. 4, pp. 114-118.
Hastings' Dictionary of the Bible, "Revelation and Inspiration,"
A. E. Garvie, Extra Vol. p. 324.
Encyclopedia of Religion and Ethics, Vol. 7, pp. 346-357.
Encyclopedia Britannica, Vol. 12, pp. 422-424.
Jewish Encyclopedia, Vol. 6, pp. 607-609.
Cyclopedia of Biblical, Theological, and Ecclesiastical Literature,
Vol. 4, pp. 611-616, including Annotated Bibliography, pp. 1707-1868.
International Standard Bible Encyclopedia, McClintock & Strong,
Vol. 3, James Orr, pp. 1473-1483.
Schaff-Herzog Encyclopedia of Religious Knowledge, Revised
1887, Vol. 2, pp. 1101-1106.

AUTHORS AND WRITINGS

Angus, Joseph—Bible Handbook, Chap. 6, pp. 101-123 1907
Barrows, E. F.—Companion to the Bible, Chap. 7, pp. 101-112, 1867
Beecher, W. J.—The Prophets of the Promise 1905
Boettner, Loraine—Inspiration of the Scriptures 1937
Briggs, C. A.—General Introduction to the Study of the Holy
                    Scriptures, pp. 110-116 1899
                    Biblical Study, (See Index "Inspiration.") ...1883
Bruce, A. B.—Chief End of Revelation 1881
Clarke, W. N.—Use of the Scriptures in Theology 1905
Cave, Alfred—Inspiration of the Old Testament 1888
Davidson, A. B.—Old Testament Prophecy 1903
Dodd, C. H.—Authority of the Bible, pp. 35-129 1929
Dods, Marcus—The Bible, Its Origin and Nature, pp. 101-129, 1929
Faunce, D. W.—Inspiration Considered as a Trend 1896
Fisher, G. P.—Nature and Method of Revelation 1890
Gaebelein, F. E.—Exploring the Bible, pp. 35-56 1929
Gardiner, J. H.—The Bible as English Literature 1906
Gardner, Percy—Historic View of the New Testament 1901
Gibson, J. M.—Inspiration and Authority of Holy Scripture, 1912

Ryle, H. E.—Canon of the Old Testament (See Index, "Inspiration") 1892

Sabatier, Auguste—Religions of Authority and the Religion of the Spirit; pp. 165-172 1904
Pauline Notion of Inspiration, pp. 305-309
Johannian Doctrine of Inspiration, pp. 309-312

Sanday, William—Inspiration, Bampton Lectures, 1893 1896
Oracles of God, Nature and Extent of Biblical Inspiration 1891

Thomas, W. H. Griffith—The Witness of History to the Inspiration of the Word Address in "God Hath Spoken" at Bible Conference 1919

Tefft, L. B.—Revelation and Inspiration in the Holy Scriptures, 1924

Van Pelt, L. R.—Introduction to the Study of the Bible, pp. 310-315 1923

Wace, Henry—Some Questions of the Day, National, Ecclesiastical, Religious 1914

Wakefield, Samuel,—Complete System of Christian Theology; pp. 71-83 1869

Warfield, Benjamin B.—Revelation and Inspiration 1927

Watson, John—Inspiration of our Faith—Sermons 1905

INDEX

INDEX

www.ingramcontent.com/pod-product-compliance
Lightning Source LLC
Chambersburg PA
CBHW060352090426
42734CB00011B/2116